# Barbados

## DIRECTIONS

WRITTEN AND RESEARCHED BY

**Adam Vaitilingam**

ROUGH
GUIDES

NEW YORK • LONDON • DELHI
www.roughguides.com

# Contents

## Introduction to

# Barbados

*Pulling in Caribbean first-timers and experienced travellers in equal measure, Barbados is justifiably one of the most popular islands in the region. Certain pleasures are quite obvious – the delightful climate, the gorgeous blue sea and brilliant white sandy beaches – but an engaging blend of cultures and a balanced approach to development help set it apart from similar sun-drenched destinations.*

◄ Beaked Heliconia

For more than three centuries Barbados was a British colony and, perhaps unsurprisingly, it retains something of a British feel: the place names, the cricket, horse-racing and polo, Anglican parish churches and even a hilly district known as Scotland. But the Britishness can be exaggerated, for this is a distinctly West Indian

## When to visit

For many visitors Barbados's tropical climate is its leading attraction – hot and sunny year-round. The weather is at its best during the high season from mid-December to mid-April, with rainfall low and the heat tempered by cooling trade winds. Things can get noticeably hotter during the summer and, particularly in September and October, the humidity can become oppressive. September is also the most threatening month of the annual hurricane season, which runs from June through October, though it's worth bearing in mind that, on average, the big blows only hit about once a decade.

country, covered by a patchwork of sugarcane fields and dotted with tiny rum shops. Calypso is the music of choice, flying fish the favoured food, and influences are as likely to emanate from America as from Europe. Meanwhile the people of Barbados, known as Bajans, are as warm and welcoming as you'll find anywhere.

Among the more traditional attractions are the island's evocative planta-tion houses, colourful botanical gardens, and proud military forts and signal stations. The capital Bridgetown makes for a lively place to visit, with an excellent national museum and great nightlife in its bars and clubs. Then there are the beaches, from the often-crowded strips such as Accra Beach and Mullins Bay to tiny but superb patches of palm-fringed sand like Bottom Bay in

A typical Barbados sunset

the southeast. And all around the island you can find first-rate food and drink; particularly delightful are the many bars and restaurants that overlook the ocean.

Despite the hordes of visitors who descend on the island, development has mostly been discreet, with many of the facilities owned by Bajans, and a distinct lack of private beaches or signs of the American fast-food franchises that blight other islands in the region. Admittedly, there are areas on both the south and west coasts where tourism is utterly dominant and Bajans massively outnumbered by European and American visitors. But, if you want to, it's easy to get away from it. Jump in a bus or a rental car and see the rest of the island: the sugar-growing central parishes, the thinly populated and little-explored north, and the ruggedly beautiful east coast, where you can hike for miles along the beach with only sea birds and the occasional surfer in sight.

The careenage, Bridgetown

## ›› BARBADOS AT A GLANCE

▶ Broad Street, Bridgetown

coast is the island's main resort area. Swarming with people but rarely feeling crowded, there are plenty of fantastic white sand beaches and enough hotels and restaurants to cater for a small army.

### Bridgetown
Easily the busiest and most populated place on the island, Bridgetown is the nation's capital. Lively, colourful and buzzing with the activities of city life, the place is mostly modern and functional, and remains home to its main businesses, schools, churches, shops and markets.

### Around Bridgetown
The outskirts of Bridgetown hold some colonial and modern day treasures, from the restored military buildings that surround the Garrison Savannah – now the island's main race-track – to the rum factories that continue to churn out top-quality liquor.

### The southwest coast
Stretching east of Bridgetown towards the airport, the southwest

◀ Garrison Savannah

### The southeast coast
East of the airport the roads wind through fields of sugarcane and small villages characterized by colourful chattel houses and tiny rum shops. Once the haunt of smugglers and wreckers, the beaches of this little-developed area – from tiny Bottom Bay to

◀ Worthing, the southwest coast

wilder Harrismith Beach – are some of the finest on the island.

## The west coast

A sparkling strip of sand runs for many miles north of Bridgetown and, though dotted with the homes of the rich and famous, remains open to all. A couple of small towns stud the coast: resort-like Holetown, with its wide selection of restaurants, shops and banks, and the quiet and largely untouristed Speightstown, a one-time thriving and wealthy port.

## Central Barbados

Acre on acre of sugarcane fields cover the central parts of Barbados, interspersed with small areas of ancient forest and the odd historic or natural attraction – welcome diversions from the beach.

## The north

Many visitors make a quick tour through the north to see green monkeys at a wildlife reserve and some ruggedly set beaches,

Virgin forest, Central Barbados

where the Atlantic lashes against the precipitous cliffs and the surf flies across the breeze.

## The east coast

This is the quietest part of the island, with miles of empty beaches and crashing waves and, inland, a series of small but picturesque villages. A great place to get away from the masses.

Viewpoint along the windswept east coast

Ideas

# The big six sights

There is a handful of attractions that, taken together, will give you a fully rounded picture of what makes the country such a special place. Seeing all six of the sights listed here will take you to nearly every corner of the island, from the **colonial architecture** outside the capital city to the windswept **cliffs** along the island's Atlantic coast, and even down into its subterranean depths.

## Garrison Savannah

Fabulous Georgian architecture surrounds the old military parade ground, now home to the island's main racetrack.

▶ P. 61 ▶ AROUND BRIDGETOWN ▲

## Barbados Museum

Simply unmissable, with superb exhibits on key aspects of the island's past and present.

▶ P. 62 ▶ AROUND BRIDGETOWN ▲

## Harrison's Cave

Brave the dankness to see these magnificent caves full of eerie rock formations and limpid pools of icy water.

▸P. 104 ▸ CENTRAL BARBADOS ▲

## The view from Hackleton's Cliff

Sensational views over the east coast make this a worthy detour as you make your way around the island.

▸P. 119 ▸ THE EAST COAST ▲

## Welchman Hall Gully

Wander through this fissure in the rock and see the island's lush vegetation as the first visitors must have done.

▸P. 105 ▸ CENTRAL BARBADOS ▲

## West coast sunset

Always spectacular, whether you get to see the legendary "green flash" or not.

▸P. 85 ▸ THE WEST COAST ▼

## Swimming spots

Most visitors to Barbados head straight for the beach for a plunge in the gorgeous turquoise sea, and the most popular **beaches** get especially packed at weekends and in high season. While the west coast beaches normally see calmer seas, the frequent swells on the south coast – and particularly in the southeast – make for great fun body-surfing or just splashing around.

### Accra Beach

An action-packed beach, bustling with vendors and sun-worshippers from sun-rise to sunset.

▸ P. 67 ▸ THE SOUTHWEST COAST ▲

### Miami Beach

Head to this protected little bay to lounge in the sea or chill with a book under the casuarina trees.

▸ P. 71 ▸ THE SOUTHWEST COAST ▲

## Crane Beach

A little remote, but a clear contender in the list of best Caribbean beaches.

▸ P. 79 ▸ THE SOUTHEAST COAST ▲

## Dover Beach

This long stretch of powdery sand on the south coast is good for light body surfing almost year-round.

▸ P. 70 ▸ THE SOUTHWEST COAST ▼

## Mullins Beach

Famous for its crowded beach bar, this splendid strip is located up in the northwest near Speightstown.

▸ P. 92 ▸ THE WEST COAST ▼

## Paynes Bay Beach

Paynes Bay is close to Bridgetown and a firm favorite with families escaping the city.

▸ P. 85 ▸ THE WEST COAST ▲

## Colonial Barbados

Barbados has a rich colonial heritage. The British, who ruled Barbados for over three centuries, left behind a fascinating architectural trove, including many **churches**, military **forts** and signal stations, and grand **plantation houses**. But the colonial legacy is not limited to fine British buildings: the brightly coloured **chattel houses**, in particular, are an enduring testimony to the ingenuity of the Barbadian people.

### Gun Hill Signal Station

The most impressive of the military communication centres that were built after the island's only major slave uprising.

▸ P. 102 ▸ CENTRAL BARBADOS ▲

### St Nicholas Abbey

The oldest residence on the island, dating back to the earliest days of colonial settlement.

▸ P. 112 ▸ THE NORTH ▲

## Harford Chambers

Every country has its much-loved lawyers; here they're housed in seventeenth-century splendour.

▶ P. 56 ▶
**BRIDGETOWN** ▶

## Tyrol Cot

This magnificent house was formerly home to two of the island's prime ministers.

▶ P. 65 ▶ **AROUND BRIDGETOWN** ▼

## Chattel houses

Just a great invention – the portable home.

▶ P. 71 ▶ **THE SOUTHWEST COAST** ▲

## Codrington College

Longstanding theological college, founded with the fortunes made from the sugar plantations that once stood here.

▶ P. 115 ▶ **THE EAST COAST** ▼

## Outdoor activities

Dragging yourself away from the sand and sea won't be easy during a stay on Barbados, but there are plenty of **outdoor activities** waiting if you do. More and more of the old sugarcane fields are being given over to new pursuits, from clay pigeon shooting to equestrian sports to golf, while the island's natural splendour offers good opportunities for hiking and biking.

### Bird-watching in Graeme Hall Swamp

This little-visited part of the island is ideal for a short spot of twitching.

▸ P. 68 ▸ THE SOUTHWEST ▲

## Parasailing

Fly high above it all for an exhilarating view of the island.

▶ **P. 138 ▶ ESSENTIALS** ▼

## Barbados Golf Club

Unlike other courses on the island, a completely unpretentious place open to all for some excellent golf.

▶ **P. 139 ▶ ESSENTIALS** ▼

## Cycling with Bonnie Cole-Wilson

Stick to the relatively flat south coast and you'll find cycling the island a breeze.

▶ **P. 139 ▶ ESSENTIALS** ▲

## Hiking in the Scotland district

Take to the hills on foot in this ruggedly beautiful area and leave the masses behind.

▶ **P. 119 ▶ THE EAST COAST** ▲

# Gourmet restaurants

Barbados has some of the finest **restaurants** in the Caribbean, showcasing great chefs and cuisine from around the world and superb **local ingredients**, particularly those freshly pulled from the ocean. Most of the classy places are along the west coast – often with spectacular locations overlooking the sea – and new spots pop up every season.

## Mango's

Not as famous as some of its west coast peers, but the seafood here is just sensational.

▶ P. 99 ▶ THE WEST COAST ▼

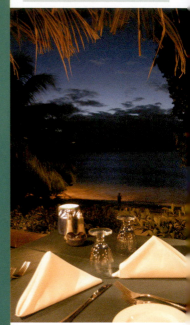

## Lone Star

Flaming torches and famous faces mark this trendy dining spot, with prices ranging from reasonable to stratospheric.

▶ P. 99 ▶ THE WEST COAST ▼

## Daphne's

A welcome and elegant newcomer to the west coast; Italian–Barbadian cuisine at its best.

▸ P. 98 ▸ THE WEST COAST ▲

## Zen

Splash out on classic Japanese and Thai cuisine and relish the immaculate vantage point high above Crane Beach.

▸ P. 84 ▸ THE SOUTHEAST COAST ▼

## The Cliff

A magnificent cliff-top location, and dependably excellent food and service.

▸ P. 98 ▸ THE WEST COAST ▼

## Josef's

As it has been for years, the finest restaurant on the south coast, with a superb location by the sea.

▸ P. 76 ▸ THE SOUTHWEST COAST ▼

## Barbados gardens

Although the virgin forest that once blanketed Barbados was largely cleared decades ago to allow planters to grow sugarcane, small tracts do remain, giving a glimpse into the island's original state. Elsewhere, you'll find vibrant flower-filled **botanical gardens** created with enormous care and attention – seldom crowded with human visitors, but often teeming with colourful birdlife.

### Casuarina Beach Club gardens

The finest hotel landscaping on the island, just a stone's throw from the beach.

▸ P. 72 ▸ THE SOUTHWEST COAST   ▾

## The Flower Forest

A converted sugar plantation, now sprawling with flowers, shrubs and a variety of palms.

▶ P. 106 ▶ CENTRAL BARBADOS ▼

## Turner's Hall Woods

The ancient silk cotton trees are the highlight in this small piece of original forest.

▶ P. 107 ▶ CENTRAL BARBADOS ▲

## Orchid World

If the thousands of orchids can't whet your appetite for these exotic blooms, nothing can.

▶ P. 104 ▶ CENTRAL BARBADOS ▼

## Andromeda Botanical Gardens

Beautifully landscaped gardens of local and imported flora, constructed with intricate care over the last half century.

▶ P. 120 ▶ THE EAST COAST ▲

## Churches and synagogues

The influence of the first European settlers is evident in Barbados's many **churches**, with the main parish churches – as well as the **synagogue** in Bridgetown – dating from the early colonial days of the mid-seventeenth century. From the elegant cathedral in Bridgetown, or the small churches scattered across the island, you'll find something to tweak your interest, whether it's hand-carved detail, atmospheric cemeteries or lovely cliff-top views.

### St James's Parish Church

Probably the prettiest of Barbados's religious buildings, rebuilt on the site of the original church.

▶ **P. 90** ▶ **THE WEST COAST** ▼

### St Peter's Parish Church

Impeccably restored after a recent fire, St Peter's is one of the main landmarks in Speightstown.

▶ **P. 93** ▶ **THE WEST COAST** ▼

## The synagogue

Located out in Bridgetown's oldest section, the Jewish synagogue preserves a slice of the island's early history.

▶ P. 56 ▶ BRIDGETOWN ▲

## Christ Church Parish Church

The stories of ghoulish happenings in the Chase family vault lend this place a slightly haunted air.

▶ P. 71 ▶ THE SOUTHWEST COAST ▼

## St Michael's Cathedral

This impressive Bridgetown cathedral is the island's main place of worship.

▶ P. 54 ▶ BRIDGETOWN ▼

## St John's Parish Church

The graveyard here is believed to be the burial site of the final surviving descendant of Emperor Constantine XI.

▶ P. 118 ▶ THE EAST COAST ▼

## Rum and sugar

The old English expression "as wealthy as a planter" holds true for the **plantations** of Barbados, which certainly brought huge riches to its sugar barons as well as great misery to the thousands of slaves and indentured labourers who toiled in the fields and in the boiling-houses. Although **sugar** has declined in importance since then, the island's main festival of Cropover still celebrates the end of the harvest, while **rum** – a byproduct of sugar – remains a vital export and a great source of pleasure for Bajans and tourists alike.

### Morgan Lewis Sugar Mill

The only working sugar mill on the island, tucked away in the quiet northeast.

▸ **P. 112** ▸ **THE NORTH** ▲

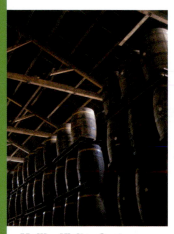

### Malibu Visitor Centre

This is where the renowned rum is made; when you've seen (and tasted) enough, the beach is great, too.

▸ **P. 65** ▸ **AROUND BRIDGETOWN** ▲

## Mount Gay Rum Factory

Just the aroma of rum will have you reeling, before you've gone anywhere near the free snifter.

▸ P. 64 ▸ AROUND BRIDGETOWN ▲

## Sir Frank Hutson Sugar Museum

A worthy testament to the island's long-standing source of wealth.

▸ P. 91 ▸ THE WEST COAST ▲

## The Foursquare Rum Factory and Heritage Park

Modern hi-tech factory with all the latest equipment and even its own little art gallery.

▸ P. 81 ▸ THE SOUTHEAST COAST ▼

## Bars and lounges

One of the island's most enjoyable features is its diverse collection of tiny **rum shops**, dotted across the island, where the big issues of the day are debated over a cold Banks beer or a half bottle of rum and a game of dominoes. On the coast, there are surprisingly few places that cater solely for drinkers – almost everywhere has food as its primary focus – but the good bars are well worth hunting out.

### Upstairs at Olive's

Mellow, comfortable bar in the heart of Holetown – the perfect place to end the evening.

▸ **P. 100** ▸ THE WEST COAST ▾

### Nelson's Arms

Horatio Nelson is still a hero at this long-standing pub, even if they're not sure what to do with his statue in town.

▸ **P. 60** ▸ BRIDGETOWN ▾

## Local rum shops

Polish up your knowledge of cricket and dominoes for a session with the locals.

▶ P. 133 ▶ ESSENTIALS  ▲

## The Ship Inn

Probably the busiest bar on the south coast, particularly when there's a band in the house.

▶ P. 78 ▶ THE SOUTHWEST COAST  ▼

## Whistling Frog Sports Pub

Chilled-out sports bar, with casual drinking and dining and TVs beaming in the latest games.

▶ P. 77 ▶ THE SOUTHWEST COAST  ▼

## Hidden beaches

You rarely have to stray far to find a **quiet beach** in Barbados. Some of the best are tucked away in the less touristed southeast – often small, secluded and studded with swaying palm trees – and if you're lucky you may get them to yourself for the day. On the east coast, too, where the surf and tides can make swimming dangerous, the beaches are often deserted and ideal for a solitary stroll.

### Bathsheba

A long brown swathe of deserted beach cherished by sea birds and surfers.

▸ P. 121 ▸ THE EAST COAST ▲

### Long Beach

A sprawling beach, not the prettiest but definitely the best place to hunt for driftwood.

▸ P. 72 ▸ THE SOUTHWEST COAST ▲

### Harrismith Beach

This wild but picturesque place is ideal for setting up a picnic for two away from the crowds.

► P. 81 ► THE SOUTHEAST COAST ▲

### Bottom Bay

This stunning white-sand beach is a photographer's dream.

► P. 81 ► THE SOUTHEAST COAST ▼

### Martin's Bay

Completely off the tourist track, this peaceful bay often sees the local fishing fleet pulled up on the sands.

► P. 117 ► THE EAST COAST ▲

### Cove Bay

Gorgeous little beach in the northeast where the occasional hustler won't spoil its appeal.

► P. 113 ► THE NORTH ▲

## Indulgent Barbados

Though you can no longer blow a fortune by flying in on Concorde, there are plenty of other opportunities to spend your packet on a bit of **luxury**. With Barbados pulling in its share of the mega-rich, five-star hotels and restaurants abound, and charter boats, planes and helicopters await to whisk passengers off on a private tour of the island or its neighbours.

### Charter boats for deep-sea fishing

Head out to sea to hunt down marlin, swordfish and barracuda on your own private charter.

▸ P. 138 ▸ ESSENTIALS ▼

### Helicopter tour

You're in for a whirlwind tour of all the sights of Barbados in just a few minutes.

▸ P. 129 ▸ ESSENTIALS ▼

## Brunch at La Mer

Hangover or not, the magnificent Sunday brunch here will get you back on your feet.

▶ P. 99 ▶ THE WEST COAST ▲

## A night at Lone Star hotel

With the waves crashing a few feet from your verandah, you can't beat this for romance.

▶ P. 96 ▶ THE WEST COAST ▼

## Cocktails at Sandy Lane

Hob-nob with the rich and famous at the legendary and spectacularly revamped west coast hotel.

▶ P. 88 ▶ THE WEST COAST ▼

## Island-hopping

Escape to one of the nearby islands, such as Grenada or Mustique (pictured), if only for a day.

▶ P. 129 ▶ ESSENTIALS ▼

# Crafts and souvenirs

The island isn't famed for its **crafts**, but visitors will find an abundance of eye-catching items to take home as mementos of their stay. The main streets of Bridgetown regularly draw flocks of cruise ship passengers in search of gifts and bargains, while elsewhere on the island particularly good souvenir-hunting options can be found around Holetown on the west coast.

### Duty-free shops on Broad Street

Compete with the cruise ship hordes in spending on low-cost liquor and jewellery.

▶ P. 57 ▶ BRIDGETOWN ▲

### Chattel House Village

Sniff out gifts for the folks back home at this pretty little chattel house estate.

▶ P. 89 ▶ THE WEST COAST ▲

## Pelican Village

The best range of souvenirs on the island is found in this attractive complex west of Bridgetown.

▶ P. 58 ▶ BRIDGETOWN ▼

## Earthworks Pottery

Browse pieces from the pottery's factory, as well as handcrafted items made by the potters up on nearby Chalky Mount.

▶ P. 87 ▶ THE WEST COAST ▼

## Shell Gallery

Beautiful collection of shells, sold individually or in cleverly crafted works of art.

▶ P. 92 ▶ THE WEST COAST ▲

# Barbados after dark

Barbados may not be a major player in the Caribbean music scene, but its handful of **nightclubs** make up in enthusiasm and buzz what they may lack in numbers. You'll find most of the action on the south coast, particularly around St Lawrence Gap, where venues lay on great sounds after the sun goes down, while for many young visitors an evening's clubbing in Bridgetown's The Boatyard ranks among the highlights of their trip.

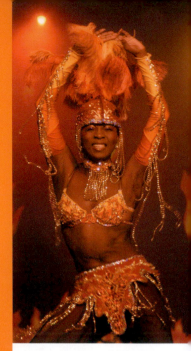

## Bajan Roots and Rhythms at the Plantation Theatre

A lavish evening of traditional Barbadian music and dance complements a tasty supper.

▶ P. 78 ▶ THE SOUTHWEST COAST ▲

## Reggae Lounge

Jamaican reggae, old and new, played with respect at this mellow little south coast club.

▶ P. 78 ▶ THE SOUTHWEST COAST ▲

## McBride's Pub

Irish pub that pulls in a good crowd every night, especially when there's a band playing.

▶ P. 77 ▶ THE SOUTHWEST COAST ▲

## The Boatyard

Whether it's live or canned music, this great beachfront club is always buzzing.

▶ P. 60 ▶ BRIDGETOWN ▼

## Club Xtreme

The latest, trendiest and probably the loudest addition to the island's late night scene.

▶ P. 78 ▶ THE SOUTHWEST COAST ▲

# water sports

The confirmed beach addict and the **water-sports** fanatic are equally at home in Barbados, where the beaches are appealingly varied and numerous operators offer a wide range of ocean-based activities. You could easily spend a week exploring all the options and, thanks to the competition, prices are generally reasonable. For diving and snorkelling trips, in particular, operators will often arrange to come and collect you from your hotel.

## Diving

Whether you're diving on a shipwreck or a reef, the fish and the coral will have you reeling in awe.

▸ P. 136 ▸ ESSENTIALS ▼

## Surfing in the soupbowl

This surfing paradise on the quiet east coast boasts some spectacular surf action.

▶P. 121 ▶ THE EAST COAST ▲

## Snorkelling

Look out for turtles on the west coast, or head out on a boat trip for some great coral heads.

▶P. 91 ▶ THE WEST COAST ▼

## Windsurfing at Silver Sands

The fair winds that blow here draw windsurfers from all over the world.

▶P. 72 ▶ THE SOUTHWEST COAST ▼

## Kayaking

If paddling about in the sea is more your speed, check out the kayak rental at The Boatyard in Bridgetown.

▶P. 138 ▶ ESSENTIALS ▼

## Bajan specialities

Whatever you do in Barbados, be sure to try some of the island's speciality **food** and **drink**. Local breweries and distilleries churn out top notch beers and rums, while an innovative local culinary tradition means that you can sample some superb dishes that you've never seen before – just bear in mind that you may have to hunt them out as many restaurants don't serve them.

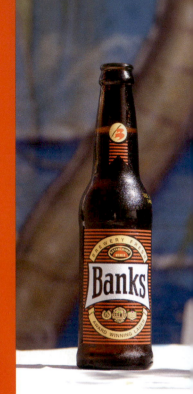

### Banks beer
Known as the Beer of Barbados, and available everywhere.

▶ P. 133 ▶ ESSENTIALS ▲

### Breadfruit
An island staple for centuries, courtesy of Captain Bligh of the Bounty.

▶ P. 133 ▶ ESSENTIALS ▼

## Cou-cou

OK – corn meal and okra may not sound like haute cuisine, but this is quite superb. *Brown Sugar* is one of the many places that serve it.

▶ P. 66 ▶ AROUND BRIDGETOWN ▲

## Pudding and souse

Don't ask what's in it – just sit back and enjoy some of the finest of the local food.

▶ P. 100 ▶ THE WEST COAST ▲

## A bottle of Mount Gay extra old rum

Let everyone else drink the basic white stuff in their cocktails; this one is for the true aficionado.

▶ P. 64 ▶ AROUND BRIDGETOWN ▶

## Barbados calendar

Bajans will use any excuse to put on a party, and there is no shortage of opportunities during the year. Traditional **festivals** celebrate matters as diverse as the local fishing fleet or the end of the sugar harvest; more modern additions to the calendar include a great festival of classical music at Holders House. International cricket matches remain one of the highlights of the year for many Bajans, notwithstanding the recent dip in form of the regional team, and the island slows down dramatically when there's a game on.

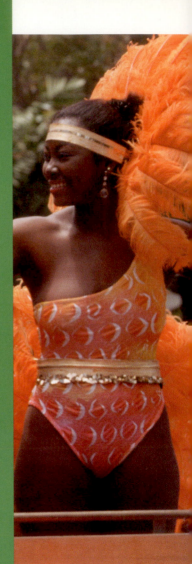

### Holetown Festival

Lively parades, street performers and stalls mark this week-long festival celebrated each February in Holetown.

▶ P. 135 ▶ESSENTIALS ▲

## Test cricket

Always a major crowd-puller, with Bajans sometimes outnumbered by supporters of the visiting team. Catch a match at the main cricket ground on Barbados, Kensington Oval.

▸ P. 59 ▸ BRIDGETOWN ▾

## Crop Over

Simply the best of the Barbadian festivals, and among the finest of carnivals in the Caribbean.

▸ P. 134 ▸ ESSENTIALS ▾

## Barbados Jazz Festival

Cool sounds float across the island during this mellow week in January.

▸ P. 134 ▸ ESSENTIALS ▲

## Casual dining

Although Barbados has no lack of places catering for the well-to-do, you don't have to be rolling in money to enjoy the island's **culinary** offerings. Delicious food at very reasonable prices can be found in many parts – though particularly in Bridgetown and the south coast resorts – from the occasional roadside vendor selling mouthwatering snacks to the bustling street markets and inexpensive restaurants and cafés.

### Fairchild Street public market

Fresh, colourful produce turned out by smallholdings across the country.

▶ P. 55 ▶ BRIDGETOWN

### Roti Hut

Simple and delicious Trinidadian rotis stuffed with a variety of fillings; take one away and snack on the beach.

▶ P. 76 ▶ THE SOUTHWEST COAST

## Coconut sellers

Let the guys chop the top off with a machete, then suck down the refreshing juice.

▶ P. 89 ▶ THE WEST COAST ▼

## Vendors in St Lawrence Gap

Cheap and satisfying jerk chicken and other snacks fresh off the grill.

▶ P. 70 ▶ THE SOUTHWEST COAST ◀

## Fisherman's Pub

Café, bar, music venue, tourist information centre – just a great all-round place to hang out.

▶ P. 98 ▶ THE WEST COAST ▲

## The Bay Garden

Don't miss a trip here for great atmosphere and some of the best fish on the island.

▶ P. 71 ▶ THE SOUTHWEST COAST ▼

# Barbados wildlife

Most of Barbados's interesting **wildlife** can be found offshore, beneath the waves. Scuba-diving is, of course, the best way to see the reef fish, but snorkellers can spot some colourful coral, fish and turtles in shallow areas off the west coast. On land, there's little by way of indigenous wildlife, but some species – like the canny green monkeys – have made their way here over the centuries, often as stowaways on sailing ships.

### Green monkeys

Visit the wildlife reserve to see these playful animals; just keep a tight grip on your handbag.

▶ P. 108 ▶ THE NORTH ▲

### Reef fish

Forget Finding Nemo, this is the real McCoy – playful schools of rainbow-coloured critters.

▶ P. 91 ▶ THE WEST COAST ▲

## Blue marlin

Join a charter boat trip for a chance to hook the most magnificent of the billfish prowling the deep offshore waters.

▸ P. 138 ▸ ESSENTIALS ▲

## Hummingbirds

More tiny than you'd expect but surprisingly nifty, beating their wings up to seventy times a second.

▸ P. 120 ▸ THE EAST COAST ▼

## Turtles

Prehistoric-looking, perhaps, but the most graceful creatures in the sea.

▸ P. 92 ▸ THE WEST COAST ▲

## Bajan oddities

Although it is one of the best-known islands in the Caribbean, not everything that you'll find on Barbados is quite as you would expect. Keep your eyes peeled for the unusual, from the **stiltman** and his entourage of shaggy bears, who entertain the crowd at cricket matches in Bridgetown, to one of the region's more obscure sports – **road tennis** – as well as a tasty, aerodynamic treat.

### Atlantis Submarine

Dive beneath the waves for a close-up look at marine life that doesn't entail you getting wet.

▶ P. 137 ▶ ESSENTIALS

## Flying fish

Impossible to miss; every restaurant seems to feature this national symbol.

▶ P. 133 ▶ ESSENTIALS ▲

## Harry Bayley Observatory

Check out the constellations in the clear Barbadian night sky on a hilltop not far from the capital.

▶ P. 69 ▶ THE SOUTHWEST COAST ▶

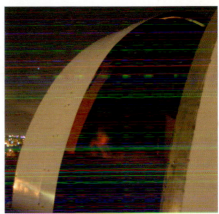

## Road tennis

Bizarre but utterly addictive game, played on flat roads throughout the island.

▶ P. 106 ▶ CENTRAL BARBADOS ◀

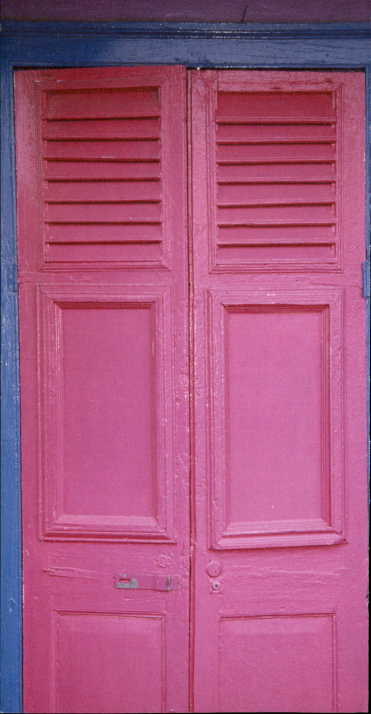

# Places

# Places

# Bridgetown

**With a gorgeous location beside the white sand beaches of Carlisle Bay, busy, modern Bridgetown is the capital and only city of Barbados. One of the oldest cities in the Caribbean, it was founded in 1628 by a tiny group of British settlers around a protected inlet known as the Careenage, still the centre of activity today though now a parking place for numerous sleek yachts. Parliament, bustling shops and a couple of smart restaurants can all be found in the immediate vicinity, while the island's main religious buildings are within five minutes' walk of here – the city itself won't take more than half a day to explore.**

## National Heroes Square

The capital's tiny main square, known for over a century as Trafalgar Square, was given its present name in 1999, though a bronze statue of Admiral Horatio Nelson still stands here. In the early nineteenth century, Barbados – like all the British West Indian islands – was under threat from Napoleon's strong Caribbean-based navy. Admiral Horatio Nelson, commanding a British fleet in pursuit of the French, stopped briefly on the island in June 1805, just four months before he was killed at the Battle of Trafalgar. In gratitude, the Barbadian parliament granted funds for a statue by the British sculptor Richard Westmacott, which was erected in 1813. The statue, however, has been deemed incongruous in the modern era

▲ SIR GARFIELD SOBERS STATUE

and the government eventually fell in with the sentiments of local calypsonian Mighty Gabby

## Getting there and getting around

Fast, efficient **buses and minibuses** run to the city from points all over the island. If you're coming from the south coast, these pass the Garrison area before terminating beside the Fairchild Street bus station. Coming from the west coast, most make their final stop at the corner of James and Tudor streets just north of the city centre. If you're driving into Bridgetown, you'll have to negotiate a slightly tricky one-way system, but there are plenty of safe, inexpensive areas to park right in the town centre. Once you're there, the central sights are easily seen **on foot**.

Eating & drinking

0          100 m

— whose *Take Down Nelson* was a massive hit — and agreed that it would be more appropriate to "put up a Bajan man" in his place. With the government's declaration of ten National

Heroes — among them cricketing genius Sir Garfield Sobers (who has his own grand bronze statue at the entrance to town), slave leader Bussa and politicians Sir Grantley Adams

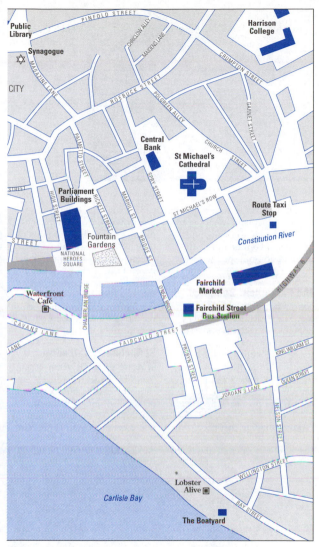

and Errol Barrow – it seems
certain that a statue of one of
the ten will eventually replace
Nelson in the square.

## The war memorial and the Fountain Gardens

East of the National Heroes
Square is an obelisk
commemorating the Barbadians
who died in World War I,

▲ THE FOUNTAIN GARDENS

houses the High Court. The present Gothic Revival buildings, put up in the 1870s, surround an arcaded courtyard and a church-like clock tower completes the ensemble. If you're in town while

behind which the tiny, well-kept Fountain Gardens are home to an ornamental fountain, put up in 1865 to commemorate the introduction of piped water to the capital.

### The Parliament Buildings

Open during parliamentary sessions only. The Parliament Buildings hold the island's two houses of parliament, the assembly and the senate. Established in 1639, Barbados's parliament is one of the oldest in the world. In its early years it met in a series of taverns and private homes, before moving to the eighteenth-century building that now

parliament is meeting you are free to watch from the public gallery provided you're properly dressed (no shorts). Inside the debating chamber, on the upper floor of the east wing, a series of stained glass windows depict thirteen British sovereigns, starting with James I and including Oliver Cromwell and a very young Queen Victoria.

### St Michael's Cathedral

St Michael's Row. Daily 9am–4pm. Free. This large, red-roofed cathedral is the country's principal Anglican place of worship. A stone church was first erected here in 1665, but

▲ THE PARLIAMENT BUILDINGS

## Bridgetown's bridges

Two **bridges** cross the Careenage, linking north and south Bridgetown as they have for centuries, though the old, rickety wooden bridges have now been replaced in more durable concrete. Nearest the sea, the Chamberlain Bridge commemorates British Colonial Secretary Joseph Chamberlain's role in securing financial aid for the island's sugar industry in 1900. In front of the bridge stands the Independence Arch – erected in 1987 to celebrate the 21st birthday of Barbadian independence – which carries the national flag, motto and pledge of allegiance. A stone's throw away, the Charles Duncan O'Neal Bridge remembers the man who founded the country's first political party, the Democratic League, in 1924.

the present building mostly dates from 1786 and was consecrated as a cathedral in 1825, when Barbados got its first bishop. It's a spacious, airy place, with a large barrel roof, and incorporates some fine mahogany carving in the pulpit and choir. The walls are decorated with a series of monumental sculptures, most notably the relief in the choir dedicated to the city's first bishop, William Hart Coleridge, while the Lady Chapel, added in 1938 at the eastern end, is splashed with colour from its stained glass. The cathedral's sprawling churchyard is the resting-place for many of the island's most prominent figures, including the first premier Sir Grantley Adams and his son Tom Adams; if you're there in spring you may be lucky enough to catch it with the red frangipani trees in full bloom.

### Central Bank

Spry Street. The nondescript modern building that towers behind St Michael's Cathedral is the island's Central Bank, at eleven storeys the tallest edifice in Barbados; it also holds the country's main concert venue, the Frank Collymore Hall, named after the great Barbadian poet, author, actor and journalist.

### Fairchild Street public market

Beside the bus concourse. The Fairchild Street public market is one of the city's two main food markets. Not quite as lively as in its heyday, the place is still worth a visit – particularly if you're here on a Saturday – for its colourful and varied produce brought in from around the island.

▼ MARKET PRODUCE

▲ ASWAD MAN SHOP

## Queen's Park

Park house daily 10am–1pm &
2–6pm. Free. Five minutes' walk
east of the city centre brings
you to Queen's Park, a large
open space that's a combination
of public park and carefully
tended sports pitches. Its main
feature is the classically
Georgian Queen's Park House,
built in 1783 as a residence for
the general commanding the
British armed forces in this part
of the Caribbean, and
continuing in that role until the
British garrison left the island
in 1905. Today the house serves
as an art gallery with changing
exhibitions of mostly local art,
and occasionally hosts theatre
performances. Standing in front
of the house is an ancient
baobab tree, eighteen metres in
circumference.

## The Old City

A maze of narrow lanes linking
the main roads above the
Parliament Buildings mark the
city's earliest sections.
Bridgetown's oldest surviving
building is probably the
seventeenth-century attorney's
office, **Harford Chambers** (on
the corner of Lucas and James
streets), whose irregular
brickwork and classic Dutch

gables are characteristic of the
city's seventeenth-century
architectural style. Immediately
opposite, the Aswad Man Shop,
with its cast-iron first-floor
balcony projecting over the
pavement, dates from around
1840.

Heading north up Coleridge
Street – a continuation of Lucas
Street – takes you past the
gleaming white police station
and the adjacent High Court,
built in 1730 and originally
home to the city's parliament
and prison as well.

The imposing building next
door is the city's **public library**
(Mon–Sat 9am–5pm), proudly
bearing the words "Free
Library" above the grand,
columned entrance. The
Barbados parliament passed an
act providing for a free library
service in 1847, though this
building – paid for by American
philanthropist Andrew Carnegie
– was only opened in 1904.

Across the road from the
library stands an elaborate
**drinking fountain**, a gift to
the city from John Montefiore,
one of its leading Jewish traders,
in 1865. Though not as jauntily
painted as in its prime, the
fountain still has stone reliefs of
Prudence, Justice, Fortitude and
Temperance and exhortations to
the thirsty citizens of
Bridgetown to "Be sober
minded" and "Look to the
end".

## The synagogue

Synagogue Lane. Daily 10am–4pm.
Free. This pink and white edifice
was first built in 1655 and
rebuilt after hurricane damage
in 1833. Jews were among the
earliest settlers in Barbados;
many of them arrived in the
1650s to escape the Inquisition
in Brazil, bringing a knowledge

of sugar-cane cultivation that was to prove crucial in boosting the island's fledgling agriculture. In 1681 there were around 260 Jews on the island – almost five percent of the population – many of them establishing successful shops and other businesses in the area around the synagogue, on roads like Swan Street (once known as Jew Street).

By around 1900, though, a long-term decline in the sugar industry had led many of the business class to emigrate, and the country's Jewish population had shrunk to fewer than twenty people. In 1929, its congregation reduced to just one person, the synagogue was sold to a private buyer and converted into offices, and in 1983 the government acquired it by compulsory purchase, with plans to demolish it and build a new Supreme Court on the site.

However, a revitalized Jewish community – boosted during the 1930s and 1940s by refugees from Europe – persuaded the government to let them take the building back. With financial aid from Jewish groups overseas, extensive restoration has returned it to something like its original shape. The attractive interior features replicas of the original glass chandeliers and a few authentic relics as well, including some cedarwood pews from 1834 and an old alms box. A series of newspaper articles displayed on the walls describes the restoration work and recounts some of the building's history. Outside, the Jewish cemetery is one of the oldest in the Western hemisphere, with dozens of cracked tombstones – some of them dating back to the seventeenth century – inscribed in Hebrew, English and (a relic of the settlers from Brazil) Portuguese.

## Broad Street

Much of central Bridgetown is given over to shopping, with dozens of duty-free stores lined up to compete for the cruise ship dollar. The main drag is Broad Street – a duty-free paradise that runs northwest from National Heroes Square. The area has been the city's market centre since the mid-seventeenth century, and still retains some splendid colonial buildings amid the modern chaos of clothes shops, jewellery stores, fast-food joints and fruit vendors. Halfway along, the enormous, late nineteenth-century **Mutual Life Building**, with its twin silver-domed towers and exquisite cast-iron fretwork, is the most distinctive of Bridgetown's colonial-era buildings.

▲ SHOPS ON BROAD STREET

## St Mary's Church

Red-roofed St Mary's Church, at the western end of Broad Street, was built in 1827 on the site of the city's first church. It's a splendid piece of Georgian Neoclassicism, apart from the turreted tower that was tacked on several decades later. Sadly, the church is often locked, but it's worth checking out the jalousied south porch and the shady graveyard where many Bajan luminaries are buried, including Samuel Jackson Prescod (one of the National Heroes) who was, in 1843, the first non-white elected to the national parliament. A large silk cotton tree in the grounds of the church, known as the "Justice Tree", was where public hangings used to take place.

▼ ST MARY'S CHURCH

## Cheapside

West of St Mary's Church, Broad Street turns into Cheapside, where you'll find the station for buses and minibuses heading north, as well as the General Post Office and one of the city's larger public markets. Just before the market, Temple Street runs down to the waterfront past a row of wooden stalls that mark the edge of **Temple Yard**, where many of the city's Rastas have long run small businesses selling sandals and other hand-crafted leather goods, as well as their distinctive red, gold and green jewellery and headgear. The area takes its name from an early nineteenth-century masonic lodge, or temple, used by the Order of the Ancient Masons that was destroyed in the 1831 hurricane.

## Pelican Village

Five minutes' walk west along the Princess Alice Highway. The Pelican Village is an excellent shopping complex built on reclaimed land, with a small art gallery, several dozen stores selling batiks, T-shirts, paintings and other souvenirs, and a couple of snack bars. There's also an opportunity here for a free tour of the **Caribbean Cigar Company** (Mon–Fri 9am–4pm),

▲ CHAMBERLAIN BRIDGE

where you'll see the tobacco leaves hanging up to dry and cigars being boxed for the duty-free market, and you can watch potters and wood-turners at work in small studios.

### Kensington Oval

Daily 9am–4pm. Ticket and schedule information at ☎436 1397. Heading northwest on Fontabelle towards the city's shallow harbour, take the signposted right turn just before the top of the road to reach the Kensington Oval, the island's premier **cricket** ground and venue for international test matches.

Cricket devotees will want to take a look around, even if there is no game in progress. For the best view of the ground, you can climb the 3Ws stand – named after the island's three master batsmen of the 1940s and 1950s, Sir Frank Worrell, Sir Everton Weekes and Sir Clyde Walcott – or the Sir Garfield Sobers stand, named after the greatest cricketing all-rounder the world has known. A small gift shop sells cricket souvenirs, including West Indies caps and videos. For more on the game, see p.140.

## Accommodation

### Grand Barbados Beach Resort

Aquatic Gap ☎426 4000, ☎429 2400, ✉grandhtl@caribsurf.com. While the *Hilton* is being rebuilt, this is the city's only hotel of note, catering primarily to business travellers. Impersonal seven-storey hotel with 130-plus rooms (from US$140/100 in winter/summer), along with gym, sauna and massage facilities. The beach is adequate, though there's a rather monstrous pier jutting off it that holds the hotel's restaurant.

## Restaurants

### Lobster Alive

Bay Street, next to *The Boatyard* ☎435 0305. Dinner daily 6.30–9pm, lunch Mon–Sat noon–3.30pm. Popular place serving delicious seafood by the beach, such as starters of cold smoked kingfish or lobster bisque for B$20 and main courses of superb conch stew with rice or lobster salad from B$30 to B$45. You can also pick a lobster from the tank and have it cooked to order.

### Nelson's Arms

Galleria Mall, 27 Broad St ☎431 0602.
Daily 11am–3pm. Large, busy pub
in the heart of duty-free shopping land – nautically themed,
and suitably decorated with
sailors and pirates – that makes
for a decent lunch break, with
flying fish, chicken, pasta and
rotis for B$15–25.

### The Waterfront Café

The Careenage ☎427 0093. Mon–Sat
noon–3pm & 6–10pm, Sun 6–10pm.
Some of the best food in
Bridgetown, with an authentic
Caribbean flavour, served
indoors or out beside the water.
Try the excellent snapper, flying
fish or dolphin fish – from B$28
to B$48 – or, if you just want a
snack, the cutters, soups and
salads. There's live music most
evenings, normally steel pan
(Tues & Wed) and jazz (Fri &
Sat). No cover charge.

# Nightlife

### The Boatyard

Bay Street ☎436 2622. Dinner daily
6–10pm, live music 8.30pm–1am.
This hugely popular nightclub is
*the* spot if you fancy an evening's
clubbing. Live bands usually play
by the beach on Tuesdays and
Fridays (B$20–35), there's
canned music and bar-dancing
on Wednesdays, and, with the
DJs spinning records on Saturdays, a B$35 cover gets you in
and all you can drink. The
decent selection of moderately
priced food includes grilled fish,
burgers and pizza.

### Harbour Lights

Bay Street ☎436 7225. Daily
9pm–3am. This nightclub right
on the beach is normally
crowded out for the all-you-
can-drink beach parties on
Mondays, Wednesdays and
Fridays (B$30 entry).

▲ THE CAREENAGE

# Around Bridgetown

Once you've had your fill of the capital – which won't take too long – it's worth investigating some of the choicer sights **around Bridgetown** that fall within a couple of kilometres of the city centre. To the south is the historic Garrison area, where the British empire maintained its Caribbean military headquarters from 1780 to 1905. Chock full of superb Georgian architecture, it remains one of Bridgetown's most evocative districts and retains the most attractive of the island's colonial military buildings. Much of the area immediately north of Bridgetown is given over to industrial production, including a couple of rum factories that are open for tours. To the northeast is Tyrol Cot, the former home of the island's first premier, Sir Grantley Adams.

## Garrison Savannah

The centre of the Garrison area, just a couple of kilometres south of the city centre, is the savannah, a huge grassy space that once served as the army's parade ground. The military buildings – barracks, quartermaster's store and hospitals, as well as the fort itself – stand in a rough square around its outer edges, flanked by coconut palms and large mango trees. The savannah is still almost permanently active, with sports grounds and play areas bounded by the city's **racetrack**, which sees action several times a year, particularly during the island's Gold Cup horse race in March. On Independence Day (Nov 30), the island's forces – the Coast Guard, the Barbados Defence Force, and the younger cadets – maintain tradition by parading on the savannah in

▼ MAIN GUARD, GARRISON AREA

## Getting there and getting around

If you're coming to the Garrison area from the west coast, catch a **bus or route taxi** heading for the south coast via the Garrison; buses marked Bridgetown stop several kilometres short. From the south coast, all buses going to the capital will stop by the savannah. If you're in Bridgetown, you'll have to get a bus or route taxi from Fairchild Street. You'll want your own transport or a taxi to get to Tyrol Cot or the rum factories.

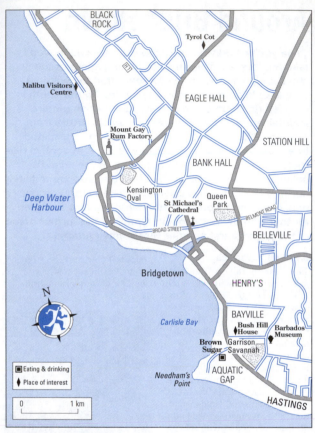

front of the island's governor-general. To the south, you can see the thick eighteenth-century walls of **St Ann's Fort** (now used by the Barbadian defence force and closed to visitors) while, just north of here, the spectacular **Main Guard** – with its tall, bright red tower and green cupola – is the area's most striking construction, though there's little to see inside. Outside, ranks of ancient but well-preserved black iron cannons point menacingly across

the savannah towards some superbly restored barrack buildings, which now serve as government offices.

## Barbados Museum

Mon–Sat 9am–5pm, Sun 2–6pm. B$11.50. Housed in the Garrison's old military prison on the east side of the savannah, this museum is stuffed with interesting and informative exhibits on the island's history and culture. A series of galleries run clockwise around an airy central courtyard that once rang with the sound of prisoners breaking stones. One of the stronger sections features immaculate little shell carvings of human figures, dating from 1000 to 1500 AD, made by Amerindians – Barbados' first inhabitants – and goes on to trace the country's evolution from a sugar-based slave society through emancipation and the early struggles of the majority black population to today's democratic, independent nation. Don't miss the small gallery on the right at the far end of the history rooms, where historic maps of the island reveal how it has changed and developed since 1627. The rest of the museum is given over to exhibits on local flora and fauna, military artefacts, prints and paintings of old Barbados,

▲ MILITARY HOSPITAL, GARRISON AREA

African crafts and decorative arts from all over the world, including glassware from England, eighteenth-century ceramics from China, Greek and Russian religious icons and some exquisite scrimshaw – pieces of ivory, bone and shell carved by sailors to while away their days at sea.

## Bush Hill House

Located on the other side of the Savannah, the Bush Hill House isn't open to the public, but it is where George Washington stayed for seven weeks during a visit to the island in 1751. Although he contracted smallpox during his stay, the future first American president was full of praise for Bajan hospitality. The illness may have been a blessing in disguise, as the immunity that he gained afterwards protected him from the smallpox epidemic that destroyed parts of the Revolutionary army during the American War of Independence. There are

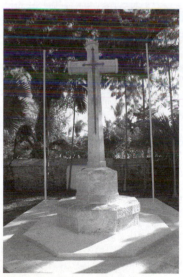

▲ NEEDHAM'S POINT MILITARY CEMETERY

grand schemes afoot to renovate the house and convert it into a museum.

## Aquatic Gap and Needham's Point

Heading back briefly towards Bridgetown on Bay Street, a left turn takes you out through Aquatic Gap – home to several expensive hotels and restaurants, including the all-inclusive *Island Inn Hotel*, housed in an old army rum store – to the tiny peninsula of Needham's Point. One of the earliest British colonial forts, Fort Charles, was built on this tiny peninsula during the 1660s and, though it fell into ruin long ago, parts of the old walls were incorporated into the grounds of the (currently under construction) **Hilton Hotel**, which, together with a large oil refinery, takes up most of the peninsula and overlooks a pleasant, bustling white sand beach popular with families at weekends. Close by is

a **military cemetery** (daily 6am–6pm; free) dedicated to the British troops who died on duty in the colony. Barbadians who died in the two world wars are also commemorated in several memorials.

## Mount Gay Rum Factory

Spring Garden Highway ☎425 8757. Mon–Fri 9am–4pm, 45min tours every 30min. B\$10. This place offers marginally the better of the factory tours, starting with a short film giving the history of the company, which first distilled rum on the island in 1703 and is reckoned to be the world's oldest surviving producer of the spirit. Mount Gay rum is actually distilled at the company's factory in the northern parish of St Lucy, but the tour shows you all the later stages in the production process, including refining, ageing, blending and bottling. The highlight of the tour is probably the vast, cool storage area,

### The story of rum

**Rum** has been a key part of Barbadian life for over three centuries, and you couldn't choose a better place to acquire a taste for the stuff. Famous as the drink of pirates and as "grog", dished out to sailors in the British navy to keep them from mutiny, it's the most potent by-product of sugar, which has been grown all over the island since the 1640s. And though production is now mechanized, the basic method hasn't changed much over the centuries.

It takes around ten to twelve tonnes of sugar cane to produce just half a bottle of rum. The juice is extracted, boiled and put through a centrifuge, producing thick, sticky molasses. This is then diluted with water, and yeast is added to get the mix fermenting. After fermentation, it's heated at the distillery, where the evaporating alcohol is caught in tanks.

In rum shops across the island, small knots of men (and occasionally women) prop up the bar beside a bottle of cheap white rum and a bottle of water, mixing their drinks to the desired strength. The choice of drink is a fine art, with a variety of bottle sizes – miniature, mini, flask, quart and pint in ascending order of size – and an equally varied selection of rums. White rum is the basis of most rum cocktails, although there are several richer, mellower options, from the golden rums of Cockspur and Mount Gay to the latter's fabulous Extra Old dark rum, best drunk neat over ice. Their darker colour is acquired from the charred American oak barrels in which they are left to mature.

▲ COCKTAILS BENEATH PALMS

crammed with barrels oozing the sweet, heady smell of rum, where the "angel's share" of evaporated rum drips from the ceiling. Afterwards, visitors can head to the bar, where the barman demonstrates how to be a rum-taster, and offers a complimentary cocktail – sit outside and sip it on the veranda overlooking the attractively landscaped gardens. There's also a small shop selling the distillery's products (although you'll find them cheaper at the duty-free shops in town) and assorted T-shirts and other paraphernalia.

### Malibu Visitor Centre

Spring Garden Highway ☎ 425-9393. Mon–Fri 9–11am & noon–4pm, tours every 30 min. B$10. The other rum tour in the area is at the Malibu Visitor Centre, adjoining the West India Rum Distillery. All of Malibu's world-famous coconut-flavoured white rum (and the less well-known lime-flavoured stuff) is manufactured here, and you get pretty much the same tour as at Mount Gay, though there isn't quite the same sense of history. The factory is right on the edge of the sea – the visitor centre even has its own little beach, where you can chill out with a complimentary cocktail after the tour – and you get a beautiful view of the turquoise sea as you explore the distilling tanks on the upper deck of the building.

### Tyrol Cot

Codringtno Hill, Mon–Fri 9am–5pm. B$11.50. The exquisite little house of Tyrol Cot was the launch pad for two of the island's most illustrious political careers. From 1929 it served as the home of Sir Grantley Adams, the first elected leader of pre-independence Barbados, and it was the birthplace of his son, Tom Adams, the nation's prime minister from 1976 until his death in 1985. The single-storey, coral block house was built in 1854 by William Farnum, one of the island's leading architects, and combines classic European and vernacular Caribbean styles. The Demerara windows, for example, are framed by Roman arches but contain adjustable double-jalousied shutters, with sloping slats that keep out rain and sun but let in light and allow air to circulate. Each of the windows also has a small but intricate cast-iron guard at its base, a flamboyant if rather eccentric addition. Inside, a collection of the family's furniture includes an ancient short-wave radio, various mahogany antiques and Sir Grantley's personal effects – among them the flag of his political dream, the Federation of the West Indies, of which he was the first and only prime minister.

Outside the house, a tiny heritage village has been built, featuring half a dozen old-fashioned chattel houses. Several showcase traditional handicrafts, with local potters, artists and basket-makers selling (and occasionally demonstrating) their crafts, and there's a typical Barbadian rum shop where you can get a drink and a bite to eat.

# Restaurants

### Brown Sugar

Aquatic Gap ☏ 426 7684. Daily 6–9.30pm. Housed in an attractive little building with iron fretwork and draped with greenery inside, this cosy place serves the best food in the Garrison area – the seafood and pasta are standouts – with prices starting around B$30. There's also a whopping buffet lunch for B$40 (Mon–Sat).

# The southwest coast

**The parish of Christ Church, in the southwest corner of Barbados, is the birthplace of tourism on the island and remains dominated by the trappings of the holiday industry. The main highway here hugs the coast, linking a string of small resorts; each consists of a fringe of white sand beach backed by a cluster of hotels, restaurants and tourist facilities. On the whole, the area is not as beautiful as the west coast, nor as lorded over by the staggering palaces of the mega-rich, but the beaches are just as fine, there are plenty of good restaurants and prices are much more reasonable.**

## Hastings

A short ride east of Bridgetown, Hastings first developed in the eighteenth century as a by-product of Britain's military development of the nearby Garrison area (see p.61). Soldiers from St Ann's Fort were quartered here – you can still see the red-brick former barracks on your left as you enter the town – and a naval hospital and the Admiral's quarters were built south of here beside the coast. More than a century later, its proximity to the capital led to Hastings being developed as Barbados's first tourist resort, and a handful of grand old hotels on the seafront still mark those glory days. Sadly, the once-attractive beach has been heavily eroded, but recent development has added a fresh splash of colour and life to the area.

## Rockley

The main attraction in this tiny, touristy village is its magnificent beach, known locally as **Accra Beach** – a great white swathe of sand, popular with tourists and local families, that can get pretty crowded at peak season and weekends. The people-watching is top-notch as hair-braiders, T-shirt and craft vendors, as well as the odd hustler, coexist with the windsurfers and sun-ripening tourists, creating one of the liveliest beach scenes on the island. Behind the beach are a couple of decent places to stay, though much of the main highway that runs through Rockley has been given over to slightly garish fast-food joints and reeks of over-development. Higher up, away from the beach and rarely seen by tourists are some of the island's most

### Getting around

Getting around the south coast is a breeze. **Buses and minibuses** run east from Bridgetown, passing through most of the tourist zones on the coast, while route taxis go as far as Silver Sands. Service stops around midnight, so you'll need a car or a private taxi after that. Getting here from the west coast is a little harder – buses run between Speightstown and Oistins, usually bypassing Bridgetown, though they're less frequent than the ones that ply the south coast.

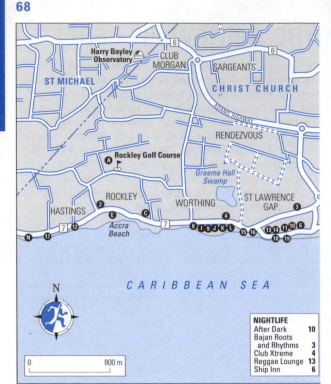

**NIGHTLIFE**

| | |
|---|---|
| After Dark | 10 |
| Bajan Roots and Rhythms | 3 |
| Club Xtreme | 4 |
| Reggae Lounge | 13 |
| Ship Inn | 6 |

exclusive residential districts, home to bankers, lawyers and other professionals working in Bridgetown.

## Worthing

Like the Victorian seaside resort in England after which it is named, this once elegant village is now tatty and faded, but its easygoing feel and handful of decent, inexpensive guest houses make it a popular target for budget travellers. There's a gleaming white beach, less crowded than Accra Beach further west but just as enjoyable, with a couple of laid-back bars, a string of vendors hanging up their T-shirts and batik prints, and

locals offering boat-trips and waverunner rentals. St Lawrence Gap, just five minutes' walk away, offers more in the way of restaurants and nightlife, but Worthing is a very likeable alternative if you want to escape the crowd. Highway 7 runs through the village, with a string of shops, banks and supermarkets on its north side and all of the accommodation to the south.

## Graeme Hall Swamp

One of the few remaining areas of mangrove swamp on the island, Graeme Hall Swamp is an important ecosystem that provides shelter for a variety of migratory birds and serves as a

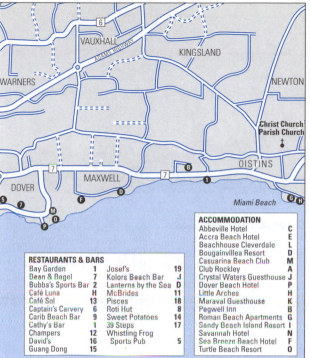

VAUXHALL

KINGSLAND

ADAMS HIGHWAY

WARNERS

NEWTON

Christ Church
Parish Church

OISTINS

DOVER

MAXWELL

Miami Beach

**RESTAURANTS & BARS**

| | | | |
|---|---|---|---|
| Bay Garden | 1 | Josef's | 19 |
| Bean & Bagel | 7 | Kolors Beach Bar | J |
| Bubba's Sports Bar | 2 | Lanterns by the Sea | D |
| Café Luna | H | McBrides | 11 |
| Café Sol | 13 | Pisces | 18 |
| Captain's Carvery | 6 | Roti Hut | 8 |
| Carib Beach Bar | 9 | Sweet Potatoes | 14 |
| Cathy's Bar | 1 | 39 Steps | 17 |
| Champers | 12 | Whistling Frog | |
| David's | 16 | Sports Pub | 5 |
| Guang Dong | 15 | | |

**ACCOMMODATION**

| | |
|---|---|
| Abbeville Hotel | C |
| Accra Beach Hotel | E |
| Beachhouse Cleverdale | L |
| Bougainvillea Resort | D |
| Casuarina Beach Club | M |
| Club Rockley | A |
| Crystal Waters Guesthouse | J |
| Dover Beach Hotel | P |
| Little Arches | H |
| Maraval Guesthouse | K |
| Pegwell Inn | B |
| Roman Beach Apartments | G |
| Sandy Beach Island Resort | I |
| Savannah Hotel | N |
| Sea Breeze Beach Hotel | F |
| Turtle Beach Resort | O |

nursery for many species of fish, which are protected from predators in the shallow waters. Beside the main road just before the turn-off to St Lawrence Gap, a damp path leading into the swamp allows you to check out the mangroves, with their huge aerial roots, and do a bit of bird spotting. Large herons nest here as well and can often be seen in the early morning and late evening.

### Harry Bayley Observatory

Open four or five nights each month, call ☎426-1317 for times. Free. Northwest of Worthing, stargazers can make for this observatory. Built in 1963, the place is headquarters of the Barbados Astronomical Society and the only observatory in the West Indies.

▲ HARRY BAYLEY OBSERVATORY

▲ FOOTBALL FIELD, DOVER

## St Lawrence Gap and Dover

As the most developed area of the south coast – with hotels, restaurants, tourist shops and vendors strung out along virtually the entire road – St Lawrence Gap and Dover are now something of a tourist enclave; you'll see few Bajans here, other than those who work in the industry and those selling **fast food** on the streets at night. Still, it remains a laid-back place with great beaches, particularly towards the eastern end of St Lawrence Gap, although erosion has taken its toll in a few spots. Most of the south coast buses and minibuses run through the area; check with the driver to make sure.

If you're here in April visit the Congaline Carnival (see p.134), when the football field at Dover normally gets taken over by food and drink stalls and crowds of people, and there's a great party atmosphere.

## Maxwell

There's not much to Maxwell, and it's easy to drive straight through on Highway 7 without noticing it. It's not a bad choice as a place to stay, though, with a couple of good hotels just to the south on the Maxwell Coast Road, a small loop off the main road. The beaches here are as good as those further west, although there's little sense of community and it can feel rather cut off in the evenings. The area is popular with windsurfers, particularly beginners and intermediates (experts head east to Silver Sands), and boards can be rented from Club Mistral (beside the *Windsurf Village Hotel*) for US$20 an hour, $55 for a half-day. Coaching is also given, though prices are exorbitant.

## Oistins

The main town along the south coast and one of its less visited parts, Oistins is linked to Bridgetown by a couple of buses, as well as route taxi 11, which continues to Silver Sands. The unusual name is a corruption of "Austin", one of the first landowners in the area and described by Ligon (an early historian) as "a wild, mad drunken fellow, whose lewd and extravagant carriage made him infamous in the island".

Sadly, he's long gone, but it's still a busy little town, dominated by a central fish market, that retains an authentic sense of Barbados before the tourist boom. The best time to visit is in the evening, when a dozen small shacks in the central **Bay Garden** restaurant (see review p.75) sell fried fish straight from the boats, and on Friday nights hundreds of people descend for a "lime", the local term for a social gathering.

In March, the annual Oistins Fish Festival celebrates the town's fishing tradition, with boat races and fish-boning tournaments.

## Christ Church Parish Church

High up north of town on Church Hill is the spooky Christ Church Parish Church. The present squat, turreted coral building is the church's fifth incarnation, the others having been destroyed by fire and hurricane. Inside, there's a modern stained-glass window behind the altar, a series of plaster reliefs along the walls and an attractive mahogany gallery at the back. The sprawling cemetery that surrounds the church is a little more interesting, with plenty of intriguing, crumbling tombs amid the frangipani and sago palms. The Chase family vault, on the church's south side, has the most peculiar history. Three times during the 1810s the vault was opened for a new burial, only to reveal that the lead coffins had mysteriously shifted from their original position. When this happened a fourth time, after the vault had been officially locked under the governor's seal, the coffins were taken out and buried elsewhere in the churchyard.

## Miami Beach

As you head east on Highway 7, take the right hand turn-off for Enterprise (a tiny village) and another right is soon signposted for the Enterprise Coast Road,

## Chattel houses

Vacant land was in short supply in nineteenth-century Barbados. Most of the tiny island was given over to sugar production, and the landless poor who worked on the plantations invariably had to live on the owner's land. Forever at risk of being evicted – in which case they would lose their homes – the workers devised a mobile house that could be taken to pieces and rebuilt elsewhere if need be. Taking their name from the legal term "chattel", meaning a moveable possession, these **chattel houses** were originally built from planks of cheap pine, imported from North America in pre-cut lengths, and rested on a foundation of limestone blocks. The facades were symmetrical, with a central door flanked by two windows; the roof was steeply gabled and the windows were jalousied to allow air to circulate and to give the house stability during hurricanes. The interiors were small, usually divided into two rooms, but as the owners garnered a bit more money, they would take the back off the house to add an identical unit or a shed with a flat roof. Another popular addition was a small veranda at the front, while owners with an artistic inclination (and the cash) would add fretwork over the doors and windows and maybe a hood above the window to keep rain out.

Few chattel houses are built today, although their attractive design remains popular and their influence can be seen in larger houses in affluent areas of Bridgetown and in tourist bars and shopping centres across the island.

offering a fabulous drive beside the sea. Upon reaching the coastal road, turn right for Miami Beach – a lovely stretch dotted with casuarina trees that marks the last protected beach before you round the headland for the exposed central and eastern beaches. You'll often find local Bajans exercising here; children playing cricket on the beach and elderly folk taking a refreshing morning swim. Alternatively, turn left past the South Point lighthouse for Silver Sands and Long Beach.

### Silver Sands and Long Beach

Famous for windsurfing, Silver Sands attracts enthusiasts from all over the world, though non-surfers come here too for the quiet, easygoing vibe. Fantastic waves roll in for most of the year and there are a handful of (pretty expensive) places where you can rent a windsurfer if you haven't brought your own. The beaches here are less busy than those further west – mainly because of the often choppy seas – but equally attractive; true to its name, Long Beach, just beyond the *Ocean Spray Apartments*, is the longest beach on the island – a huge stretch of crunchy white sand strewn with driftwood – and is often completely deserted.

# Accommodation

### Abbeville Hotel

Rockley ☎ 435 7924, ℱ 435 8502.
Friendly and easy-going little place, motel-like in design, with a small pool. The rooms (from US$55/45 in winter/summer) are simple and somewhat tired, but the setting, around a courtyard and huge bar, gives the place a welcoming feel.

### Accra Beach Hotel

Rockley ☎ 435 8920, ℱ 435 6794, ⓦ www.accrabeachhotel.com.
Attractive hotel with fifty pleasant rooms right on the island's busiest beach, featuring balconies overlooking the sea, palm trees strewn around the gardens and a giant swimming pool. Come evening there's a Polynesian restaurant and an outdoor dance floor. Rooms from US$144/185 in summer/winter.

### Beachhouse Cleverdale

Worthing ☎ 428 1035, ℱ 428 3172, ⓦ www.barbados-rentals.com.
German-managed guest house with single/double rooms starting as low as US$25/28 in winter/summer, and a communal kitchen, breakfast room, living room and spacious veranda.

### Bougainvillea Resort

Maxwell ☎ 418 0990, ℱ 428 2524, ⓦ www.barbados.org/hotels/bougainvillea. Popular with British tour groups, this 95-room hotel sits on a lovely stretch of beach and has helpful staff, several pools, free water sports, tennis courts and evening entertainment. The restaurant is only adequate, but there are plenty of dining options in St Lawrence Gap, a short taxi ride away. Rooms from US$252/147 winter/summer.

### Casuarina Beach Club

Dover ☎ 428 3600, ℱ 428 2122, ⓦ www.barbados.org/hotels/casbeach.
Big, popular and beautifully landscaped hotel with fabulous gardens beside an excellent beach, plus tennis courts, a decent pool, activities for children and adults, and one of the island's finest collections of local art. All rooms (from

## Crystal Waters Guesthouse

Worthing ☎ 435 7514. One of the best of the local guest houses – no frills, but a friendly and comfortable place, with hardwood floors, a TV lounge, a delightful veranda and a laid-back beachside bar. Excellent breakfasts, too. Rooms from US$35 year round.

## Dover Beach Hotel

Dover ☎ 428 8076, ℻ 428 2122, ⊛ www.doverbeach.com. Comfortable, easy-going place located beside a superb beach. All the rooms (from US$70 year round) have air-conditioning, some have kitchenettes, and there's a good-size pool. One of the best options in this price category. Ask for a room with a beach or pool view.

## Little Arches

Miami Beach ☎ 420 4689, ℻ 435 6483, ⊛ www.barbados.org./hotels/littlearches. Smart new place a short walk from delightful Miami Beach. The rooms are good-sized, with luxurious bathrooms and air-conditioning, though the popular restaurant and bar upstairs can make the place a bit noisy in the late evening. There's also a tiny pool and hammocks to lounge in. Rooms from US$220/160 in winter/summer.

## Maraval Guesthouse

Worthing ☎ & ℻ 435 7437, ⊛ www.maravalbarbados.com. Funky little place, popular with European backpackers, with five rooms at US$35 for a double room year round. There's a communal kitchen and eating area and you're a stone's throw from the beach.

▲ CRYSTAL WATERS GUESTHOUSE

US$195/110 in winter/summer) have self-catering facilities, and the front desk can arrange island tours, including cycle trips led by the hotel's enthusiastic owner.

## Club Rockley Barbados

Rockley ☎ 435 7880, ℻ 435 8015, ⊛ www.clubrockley.com. Popular all-inclusive village, ten minutes' walk (or a shuttle ride) from the beach, with four restaurants, several pools, good sports facilities and its own nightclub and decent nine-hole golf course (☎ 435 7873); green fees are B$60–110, with rental of clubs an additional B$20. Though there are a lot of people about, the complex's spread-out design helps keep it from feeling too crowded. All-inclusive rates from US$125 per person.

### Pegwell Inn

Welchs, just west of Oistins ☎ 428 6150. This tiny guest house is the cheapest place to stay in Barbados. The four simple rooms (from US$25 year round) all have fans and private bathrooms and, though it's beside the main road and can be a little noisy, it's only a five-minute walk to the beach.

### Roman Beach Apartments

Miami Beach ☎428 7635, ℱ428 2510. Lush bougainvillea surrounds this little group of simple apartments, five minutes' walk from Oistins and right by a secluded stretch of beach. Rooms from US$55 year round.

### Sandy Beach Island Resort

Worthing ☎ 435 8000, ℱ 435 8053. Big pink and white hotel with tennis courts, a curiously landscaped pool and regular nightly entertainment. The rooms (from US$143/100 in winter/summer) aren't up to much, and the whole place presently feels a little run down, but the beach is so good you'll be spending most of your time there.

### Savannah Hotel

Hastings ☎ 228 3800 ℱ 228 4385, ⓦwww.barbados.org./hotels/gems/sav annah. A short walk from the beach, a well-designed complex where some of the one hundred rooms (from US$337/253 in winter/summer) are housed in historic and newly renovated buildings of the Garrison. The staff are friendly and helpful, and amenities include two big pools and two restaurants as well as a fitness centre.

### Sea Breeze Beach Hotel

Maxwell ☎428 2825, ℱ428 2872, ⓦwww.barbados.org/hotels/seabreeze/index.htm. Large, nicely landscaped property with two swimming pools, a gym and some outdoor Jacuzzis by a lovely beach. The food is good, too, so those on the optional all-inclusive package are invariably well fed and contented. All rooms come with a/c, TV and fridges; studios with kitchenettes. Room from US$185/115 in winter/summer.

### Silver Rock Hotel

Silver Sands ☎428 2866, ℱ420 6982, ⓦwww.barbados.org/hotels/gems/silve rrock. Three-storey pink and

▲ SOUVENIR STAND, ACCRA BEACH

white block with 33 comfortable rooms (from US$145/120 in winter/summer), a pool and a crowd of surfer guests. There's a reasonable restaurant on site, and most rooms have kitchenettes. If you're not here for the kite- or wind-surfing, you may find the place isolated and the other guests obsessed.

### Silver Sands Resort

Silver Sands ☎ 428 6001, ℻ 428 3758. The only full-blown resort in the area, elegantly furnished with two restaurants, tennis courts, a large swimming pool and over one hundred air-conditioned rooms spread across a large area of landscaped grounds. Rooms from US$130/70 in winter/summer.

### Turtle Beach Resort

Dover ☎ 428 7131, ℻ 428 6089, ⊛ www.eleganthotels.com. Top-notch all-inclusive, with 160 decent-sized rooms, fine restaurants, good water-sports facilities and a kid's club that entertains the young ones all day long. The delightful beach outside can get a bit crowded with the hotel's guests, but it's a short walk to find a quiet space. All-inclusive rates from US$150 per person.

# Restaurants

### 39 Steps

Chattel Plaza, Hastings ☎ 427 0715. Mon–Fri noon–midnight, Sat 6pm–midnight; live music every other Sat 7.30–10pm. Fashionable and atmospheric wine bar and restaurant; the chalked-up daily specials normally include several excellent fish dishes, as well as good soups and salads. Main courses run B$27–55. Mellow live jazz every other Saturday.

### The Bay Garden

Oistins Market, Oistins. Daily 5.30–10pm. One of the most atmospheric places on the island, with several dozen stalls offering a variety of seafood from spicy conch fritters to huge plates of fried kingfish or dolphin, served with peas and rice, macaroni pie and vegetables. Prices are low: you'll be hard-pressed to pay more than B$20 a head. If you go into the covered *Fish Net* area you'll find plenty of locals tucking into equally good barbecued fish straight off the grill.

### Bean & Bagel

Dover ☎ 420 4604. Daily 7am–5.30pm. Great coffee, all-day breakfasts of bagels, pancakes and omelettes, giant muffins and tasty lunch options (lasagne, crab backs and such) have made this Internet café a favourite among those staying at the eastern end of St Lawrence Gap.

### Café Luna

*Little Arches* hotel, Miami Beach ☎ 420 4689. Daily 8am–9pm. Excellent food served on a terrace at the top of the *Little Arches* hotel (though its uncovered, so don't go if there's rain threatening). The theme is Mexican, with soft tacos and nachos on the menu, but you'll also find starters such as warm duck salad and mains including sushi, fresh fish and black bean chicken. Main courses cost around B$25–60.

### Café Sol

St Lawrence Gap ☎ 435 9531. Daily 6–11pm. Lively, often crowded Mexican place doing a roaring trade in margaritas and Mexican beers, particularly during the 6–7pm and 10–11pm happy hours. The food sometimes feels secondary to the party atmosphere, but you'll get decent and sensibly priced chicken, beef and vegetarian burritos, tacos and enchiladas (B\$20–52).

## David's

St Lawrence Gap ☎ 435 9755. Tues–Sun 6–10pm. Popular place overlooking Little Bay, serving delicious local food; main courses starting at B\$45 include pepperpot stew, rack of lamb and curried chicken. Vegetarians will find more choices here than most places elsewhere: vegetable crepes and lemon-tossed linguine, for example, for B\$45.

## Guang Dong

Main road, east end of Worthing ☎ 435 7387. Daily 11am–2pm & 6–10pm. Solid Chinese restaurant offering typical dishes of sweet and sour pork, chow mein and chop suey, from B\$15, with particularly good lunchtime combo deals for B\$16.

## Josef's

St Lawrence Gap ☎ 435 6541. Daily 6–10pm, Dec–April also noon–2pm. Both the food and the service at this elegant coral stone restaurant are as good as you'll find anywhere on the island, with candelit tables both indoors and (more romantically) down by the water's edge. Starters (B\$12–35) include fantastic shredded duck in pancakes with a coconut and red curry sauce, while among superb main courses (B\$45–95) are seared yellowfin tuna in a mango–cilantro sauce and herb-crusted rack of lamb.

## Lanterns by the Sea

At the *Bougainvillea Beach Hotel*, Maxwell ☎ 418 0990. Daily noon–2.30pm and 6.30–9pm. The best place to eat on this strip, with good local and international food including seafood specials, barbecues and an excellent buffet on Sundays. The atmosphere is relaxed and the views over the water make it a good spot for lunch or early evening.

## Pisces

St Lawrence Gap ☎ 435 6564. Daily 6.30–10pm. Cavernous but attractive waterside restaurant with a strong emphasis on seafood – catch of the day, usually snapper or dolphin, costs around B\$40; seared prawns in coconut curry sauce B\$48. Service can be rather hit-and-miss though, particularly when there's a tour group in.

## Roti Hut

Main Road, Worthing ☎ 435 7362. Mon–Sat 11am–10pm, closed Sun. Good place to munch on inexpensive rotis – options include potato rotis for B\$3.50, chicken and potato for B\$8 and shrimp for B\$9.

## Sweet Potatoes

St Lawrence Gap ☎ 428 7153. Mon–Sat 5.30–9pm. A lively and fun place with colourful decking and a long wooden bar, *Sweet Potatoes* sells itself as "good old Bajan cooking" and dishes up pretty good starters of fish cakes, marinated codfish and pumpkin and spinach fitters (B\$10–12) and main courses of jerk pork, mango chicken and stuffed flying fish (B\$32–35), all served with a choice of tasty side dishes.

## Whistling Frog Sports Pub

Dover, opposite *Escape at the Gap Hotel* ☎ 420 5021. Daily 7am–very late. Slightly faded bar-bistro serving food all day, from a buffet breakfast to lunch and supper of chicken wings, pepperpot stew or seafood caesar salad (all around B$15), though many here simply hang out with a drink watching sport on the TVs. Happy hours 6–7pm and 9–10pm.

# Bars

### Bubba's Sports Bar

Across from the *Accra Beach Hotel*, Rockley ☏ 435 6217. Daily 10am–10pm. The food is very much secondary to the entertainment here – sport from around the world shown on large and small TV screens – but you can get decent and reasonably priced burgers, chicken, steaks and sandwiches to munch while you gawp. Main courses start at B$20.

### Captain's Carvery

The Ship Inn, St Lawrence Gap ☏ 435 6961. Daily noon–3pm, 6–10.30pm. Huge, nautically themed pub, with a wide range of beers and food to go along with regular live music. All-you-can-eat buffet options for lunch and dinner specialize in roast meats and come with baked potatoes and a variety of salads. Expect to pay around B$30–40 per person.

### Carib Beach Bar

Next to *Crystal Waters Guesthouse*, Worthing ☏ 435 8540. Daily 11.30am–10pm. A lively place for a drink, especially during the early evening happy hour from 5pm to 6pm, when you'll also get reasonably priced snacks including spicy chicken wings, shrimp kebabs and fish cakes.

### Cathy's Bar

Oistins. No phone. Daily 5–11pm. This typical Bajan rum shop in the centre of the Oistins Market is a pleasant place to grab a drink and meet some of the locals before heading to the *Bay Garden* for your fish dinner.

### Champers

Hastings ☏ 435 6644. Daily 6–10pm. Attractive and friendly bar-restaurant right on the oceanfront, serving tasty steak and seafood main courses for B$20–45; there's also an excellent selection of wines.

### Kolors Beach Bar

Next to the *Crystal Waters Guesthouse*, Worthing ☏ 435 8000. Daily 11am–10pm. A lively place for a drink, especially during the early evening happy hour from 5pm to 6pm, when you'll also get reasonably priced snacks such as spicy chicken wings, shrimp kebabs and fish cakes.

▲ CARIB BEACH BAR

### McBride's Pub

St Lawrence Gap ☎ 435 6352. Daily 5pm–midnight. The inevitable Irish pub – yes, they do serve Guinness. Usually crowded with twenty-something holiday-makers, and blaring out the latest in Britpop. Bangers and mash go for B$22, Irish stew for B$28.

# Nightlife

### After Dark

St Lawrence Gap ☎ 435 6547. Daily 10pm–3am. The late night zone – a huge but cleverly laid out and atmospheric place with a dark, smoochy disco and a massive stage and dance floor out the back for the live bands who play a couple of times a week. The bar – nearly 30m long – claims to stock every liquor you can name, and the crowd is a good mixture of Bajans and tourists, all dressed up to the nines and partying until 3am. Cover charge varies.

### Bajan Roots and Rhythms

Plantation Theatre, St Lawrence Gap ☎ 428 5048. Wed and Sun 7pm. B$145 (B$80 for show only). Polished and popular show that relates, through storytelling and traditional music and dance, the history of the island since the British first landed here. Your entry fee, if you choose, gets you a Bajan buffet, drinks and transfer to the theatre.

### Club Xtreme

Worthing Main Road ☎ 228 2582. Wed, Fri & Sun 9pm–late. Brand new, cavernous and high energy club, with a superb sound system banging out the latest techno and dance as well as a big games area with pool tables and numerous arcade games.

### Reggae Lounge

St Lawrence Gap ☎ 435 6462. Daily 9pm–late. Intimate, unpretentious club with a small bar up top and concrete steps down to the open-air dance floor under the palm trees. The DJs love to play the latest Jamaican dancehall, but you'll also get "oldies" nights – Bob Marley, Jimmy Cliff, Peter Tosh – and live bands several times a week, usually Thursdays and Sundays. Cover charge varies.

### The Ship Inn

St Lawrence Gap ☎ 435 6961. Daily 9pm–1am. English pub in style, with several bars and a small, sweaty dance floor, with the most tourist-friendly bands – reggae meets rap meets Marvin Gaye. There's music every night from around 10.30pm–12.30am and bands, and a big crowd, on Tuesdays and Saturdays.

▲ HAIR-BRAIDING STALL

# The southeast coast

Tourist development has never really taken hold in the **southeast** of the island. The coastline here, in the parish of St Philip, is much more rugged than that further west, with only a handful of white sand beaches – several of them, especially Crane Bay and Bottom Bay, quite spectacular – divided from each other by long cliffs and rocky outcrops. The sea is much rougher too, with Atlantic waves crashing in all year round. Bear this in mind if you are thinking of staying here; while there are several places where you can swim safely, the pounding surf can quickly get tiring. If you're not staying, there's still a handful of attractions worth making for, including an interesting rum factory and an old plantation house. Not surprisingly, nightlife is nonexistent.

## Foul Bay

Three or four kilometres east of the airport, Foul Bay is the largest beach on this section of the coast. Access is signposted; go past the large Methodist Church beside the road in the small village of Rice and a right turn 100m further on takes you right down to the beach. It's a long, wide, white sand beach with a handful of fishing boats normally pulled up on its eastern side, and you'll find few tourists (and no food and drink facilities). The long cliffs give the place a rugged feel but it's not particularly pretty – if you're after a more picturesque "dream" beach, you may want to head for Bottom Bay, a little further east.

## Crane Beach

On the main road, the *Crane Beach Hotel* lies half a kilometre

▲ FOUL BAY

## Getting there

If you're relying on public transport, **buses** run along the south coast road as far as *Sam Lord's Castle*, passing the *Crane Beach Hotel*, though if you're heading for any of the beaches you'll need to walk down to them from the main road – which is usually around 500m.

▲ HARRISMITH GREAT HOUSE

beyond Foul Bay. This was one of the first hotels on the island, and it commands a superb site above Crane Bay. In spite of the new timeshare developments behind the hotel, it's still a fetching place and worth a look even if you're not staying (a fee of B$5 is charged for use of the facilities, though you can put it towards any food or drink you have during your visit). A long Roman-style swimming pool runs alongside the main hotel building at the top of the cliff and, beside the panoramic restaurant, two hundred steps lead down to the very pretty Crane Beach. Various writers have waxed lyrical over this beach during the last century, but hurricane damage has altered its shape and it is no longer quite as fabulous as they once claimed. On the other side of the pool, a walkway carved into the rock also winds down to the ocean – this was first cut during the 1760s to provide a discreet bathing spot for women, but is no longer in use.

## Sam Lord's Castle

Open to non-guests daily 9am–5pm. Five minutes' drive east of Crane Bay, *Sam Lord's Castle* is a large hotel, spread out above a couple of decent beaches. The place is open to anyone, though non-guests are supposed to pay an entrance fee of B$12 (redeemable at any of the hotel's

## Harrismith and Bottom Bay practicalities

To get to **Harrismith**, head out of *Sam Lord's Castle* and take the first right up to the main road, then turn right again. After 500m or so there is a right turn marked "Harrismith". Follow the road down and turn left along a rutted track just before you reach a couple of casuarina trees. At the bottom of the track is the deserted Harrismith Great House, a former hotel overlooking Harrismith Beach.

To reach **Bottom Bay**, continue along the main road past the Harrismith turn-off and the turning is signposted on the right. Park at the top of the cliffs and walk down the steps.

## Bussa's rebellion

In 1807 the British government banned the transfer of slaves from Africa to the Caribbean. While the measure had little immediate impact on the Barbadian planters, who preferred Creole slaves born on the island, it did add fuel to the growing movement for the overall abolition of slavery. In an attempt to deflect criticism, Barbadian planters made some token improvements to the slaves' conditions: women's working hours were reduced; whites could be punished for the murder of a black; and slaves were permitted to own property.

The slaves, though, knew that none of this was conceded willingly, and rumours spread claiming that emancipation had been proclaimed in Britain but was being blocked on the island. Frustration grew, and in April 1816 Barbados faced its only serious slave uprising. **Bussa's Rebellion** – named after its leader, an African-born slave who was head ranger at a plantation in St Philip – began in the south-east with attacks on property and widespread burning of the sugar fields. It quickly spread throughout the southern and central parishes, and the slaves fought several battles against the white militias and British troops. They never stood a chance: within three days the rebellion was crushed, with only a handful of white casualties but over a thousand slaves either killed in battle or executed afterwards, along with prominent free coloured supporters of emancipation. There were no further outbreaks of major violence, but the abolitionist movement in Britain grew until slavery was finally ended in 1834.

bars or restaurants) for access to it and the beach. The hotel buildings spread out around a central mansion – the "castle" – built in 1820 by Sam Lord, a legendary local crook who reputedly made his fortune from luring ships onto the nearby reef and salvaging anything of value. Though the story is questioned by local historians, there is no doubt that Lord made a lot of money from one dubious source or another and spent much of it building his home here. Parts of the house were built by craftsmen from England in the style of Windsor Castle and the downstairs rooms – all on show – are expensively furnished and decorated.

### Harrismith and Bottom Bay

Beyond *Sam Lord's Castle* are a couple of good beaches worth checking out. The first, Harrismith Beach, is overlooked by the old Harrismith Great House, with steps leading down just west of the house. It's pretty and usually very quiet here, with palms, cliffs and small caves for exploring. Surpassing it is Bottom Bay, a small sugar-white beach sandwiched between cliffs, with a backdrop of palm trees and the Atlantic waves crashing in. Few people find the place (see the practicalities box), although locals use it at the weekend and the occasional tour bus heads this way during the week.

### The Foursquare Rum Factory and Heritage Park

Mon–Thurs 10am–6pm, Fri & Sat 10am–9pm, Sun noon–6pm. B$12. Smack in the middle of sweeping fields of sugar cane, the Foursquare Rum Factory and Heritage Park is an ultra-modern rum distillery built on the site of an ancient sugar estate. The factory combines state-of-the-art design with traditional features and buildings, and the compulsory forty-minute tour is an interesting introduction to the production of sugar and its chief

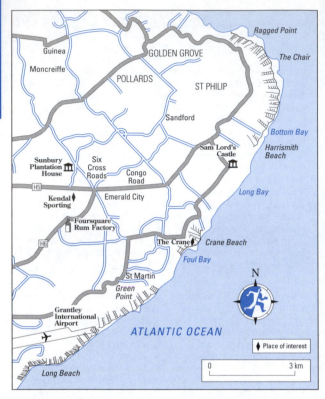

Map key labels: Ragged Point, Guinea, GOLDEN GROVE, The Chair, Moncreiffe, POLLARDS, ST PHILIP, Sandford, Bottom Bay, Sunbury Plantation House, Six Cross Roads, Congo Road, Sam Lord's Castle, Harrismith Beach, H5, Kendal Sporting, Emerald City, Long Bay, Foursquare Rum Factory, H6, The Crane, Crane Beach, Foul Bay, St Martin, Green Point, N, Grantley International Airport, ATLANTIC OCEAN, Place of interest, 0 3 km, Long Beach

by-product, rum. Tours start with a short video about Bajan rum-making and the history of the Foursquare sugar plantation, which was established in the 1640s, during the earliest days of sugar on Barbados. Moving on through the gleaming factory, guides point out the modern boilers and fermentation tanks and explain how the rum is produced. At the end of the tour, you'll get a free drink and be left in the 250-year-old foundry, a long, elegant building of thick coral stone blocks.

The place now serves as a trendy art gallery for paintings and sculptures by Bajan artists and occasional exhibitions of work from around the Caribbean. Most of the pieces are for sale, and you can also buy bottles of the ESA Field rum made in the factory. Dotted around the site are craft studios that make and sell wicker baskets, leather bags and jewellery, and stalls selling snacks and drinks.

## Sunbury plantation house

Daily 10am–5pm. B$13.80. Sunbury is one of the oldest and – for the sheer variety of furniture, artwork and colonial-era bits and pieces – most interesting of the island's great houses. The entry fee includes a guided tour of the interior, after which you're free to wander through the main rooms and around the extensive gardens, or snack at the small outdoor café.

Ownership of the sugar estate dates back to the very first settlers in Barbados, although the plantation house dates from the mid-eighteenth century. From 1835 to 1981, the plantation was owned by the family of local shipping merchant Thomas Daniel, a friend of the notorious Sam Lord (see p.81). The building was restored after being gutted by fire in 1995, and looks almost exactly as it did beforehand. Although only the walls are original, built with local coral blocks and ballast from British ships and made 50cm thick to withstand hurricane winds, the restoration brilliantly recaptures the period feel of the rooms, helped by donations of furniture and other artefacts from around the island. There is a wealth of old mahogany pieces on the ground floor, with the massive claw-footed dining table taking pride of place, while the walls are lined with prints and paintings of old Barbados. Upstairs, the bedrooms show off nineteenth-century fashions; downstairs, the cellars are stuffed with paraphernalia from traditional plantation life, including horse-drawn buggies, cooking pots, cutlery and the sad, charred relics of the 1995 fire.

## Accommodation

### Crane Beach Hotel

ⓣ 423 6220, ⓕ 423 5343, ⓦ www.thecrane.com. With a stunning setting high above Crane Bay, this once small and exclusive place has been thoroughly changed by the addition of adjoining timeshare apartment blocks. Even so, the place remains luxurious and highly recommended, with two excellent restaurants. The superb beach is reached via a long staircase. Rooms from US$330/155 in winter/summer.

▲ SUNBURY PLANTATION HOUSE

▲ CRANE BEACH HOTEL

## Sam Lord's Castle

☎ 423 7350, ⑤ 423 5918,
ⓦ www.samlordscastle.com. More
mansion-house than castle, with
a handful (and the best) of the
280 rooms in the main house
and the rest scattered around the
attractive gardens. There are
three swimming pools, as well as
tennis courts and an exercise
room, and entertainment – from
steel band music to karaoke – is
laid on nightly. All-inclusive
rates from US$90 per person.

# Restaurants

## L'Azure

*Crane Beach Hotel* ☎ 423 6220. Daily
for lunch and dinner noon–2.30pm &
6–9pm. Overlooking the bay and
serving excellent and innovative
seafood dishes, this is the main
restaurant of the *Crane Beach
Hotel* and makes for a good
lunch stop if you're in the area.
Bear in mind, though, that
prices are on the high side
(around B$45 for fish of the
day), and that the place lacks
atmosphere out of season.
Sundays see a buffet lunch with
accompanying steel pan music.

## Zen

*Crane Beach Hotel* ☎ 423 4107. Daily
for dinner 6–9pm. Classy place
serving Japanese and other Asian
cuisines, with delicious but
pricy sushi, sashimi and tempura
among the pick of the dishes.

# The west coast

The sandy beaches and warm blue waters of the sheltered Caribbean side of Barbados have made its **west coast** – the so-called platinum coast – the island's prime resort area. As a result, much of the coastline has been heavily built up with the island's top restaurants and priciest hotels, and sought-after private homes. There is, however, a smattering of reasonably priced places to stay and all of the beaches are public, many of which are worth seeking. The region has other attractions, including lively, modern **Holetown**, with its fine old church and a legion of shopping opportunities, and **Speightstown** further north, where colonial relics and picturesque old streets recall its vanished heyday as a major port.

## North to Paynes Bay

There is little sign of the hotel extravaganza to come as Highway 1 begins to carve its way up the west coast through the tiny village of Prospect. Most of the buildings here are residential and the beaches – largely bereft of tourists – are popular at weekends and holidays with families up from Bridgetown. The first of these, **Betts Rock Park** is a large, slightly scruffy beach zone with a couple of lifeguard towers and a picnic area. A better bet, if you want to swim, is **Prospect Beach**, a little further up the coast – a narrow crescent of sand, backed by manchineel trees and palms, and a calm turquoise bay. Public access is via a path just north of the all-inclusive *Escape Hotel*, and at busy times the beach can get crowded with the hotel's guests. Alternatively, head up to the beach at **Paynes Bay**, next to some of the west coast's finest restaurants and opposite the turn-off to Holders House.

## Holders House

Founded in 1993, the Caribbean's leading **festival** of classical music is now held annually in March at this gorgeous old plantation house and private home just inland from Sandy Lane Bay. If you're

---

### Getting there and getting around

It could hardly be easier to get around on the west coast. North of Bridgetown, Highway 1 runs up the coast, rarely straying more than 100m from the shoreline. Highway 2A runs parallel to it, some way inland, and offers a speedier way of getting to the north of the island.

**Buses and minibuses** ply the coast road between Bridgetown and Speightstown all day, and there are bus stops every couple of hundred metres. Services normally stop at around midnight, after which you'll need a car or private taxi. If you're coming from the south coast, look for buses marked "Speightstown" – these usually bypass Bridgetown and save you having to change buses (and terminals) in the city.

**ACCOMMODATION**

| | |
|---|---|
| Almond Beach Village | B |
| Angler's Apartments | M |
| Beachcomber Apartments | J |
| Cobblers Cove | C |
| Crystal Cove | N |
| Escape | O |
| King's Beach Hotel | E |
| Little Good Harbour | A |
| Lone Star | F |
| Sandridge Hotel | D |
| Sandy Lane | I |
| Settlers' Beach | G |
| Smuggler's Cove | L |
| Sunset Crest | H |
| Treasure Beach | K |

**RESTAURANTS & BARS**

| | |
|---|---|
| Angry Annie's | 13 |
| Back to Eden | 5 |
| Bombas | 15 |
| Carambola | 21 |
| Chattel House | D |
| The Cliff | 20 |
| Coach House | 16 |
| Crocodile's Den | 17 |
| Daphne's | 18 |
| Emerald Palm | 8 |
| Fish Pot | 1 |
| Fishermen's Pub | 3 |
| Garden Bar | M |
| La Mer | 2 |
| La Terra | 7 |
| Lone Star | F |
| Mango's | 4 |
| Marshalls | 19 |
| The Mews | 12 |
| Olive's Bar and Bistro | 11 |
| Ragamuffin's | 10 |
| Suga Suga Beauty Bar | 6 |
| Surfside Beach Bar | 14 |
| Tam's Wok | 9 |

◆ Place of interest

Six Men's Bay

Speightstown

St Peter's Parish Church

ST PETER

Mullins Bay

The Shell Gallery

Alleynes Bay

ST JAMES

Folkestone Marine Park

St James Parish Church

Sir Frank Hutson Sugar Museum

Holetown

Portvale Sugar Factory

St Thomas Church

West Coast Mall

CARIBBEAN SEA

Sandy Lane Golf Course

ST THOMAS

Chattel House Village

Sandy Lane Bay

Sunset Crest shopping area

Earthworks Pottery

Paynes Bay

Holders House

Bagatelle House

N

PROSPECT

Batts Rock Park

0          2 km

▲ ARLINGTON, SPEIGHTSTOWN

familiar with the reggae festivals of Jamaica, or Carnival in Trinidad, you may find it somewhat incongruous to find operas and classical concerts being performed in period costume outdoors under the mahogany and palm trees. But little expense is spared – quality singers and musicians are flown in specially from Britain – and the spectacular setting invests the whole thing with a magical air. The owners generally put together an imaginative schedule: attractions have included the restaging after 170 years of *Inkle and Yarico* – an eighteenth-century opera about a traditional Barbadian legend that was once all the rage in London's West End – as well as a concert by Pavarotti and, away from the classical sphere, a festival of calypso music with contributions by top performers from Trinidad and Barbados. For details, contact the Barbados Tourism Authority (☎427 2623, ☎426 4080) or Holders House direct (☎432 6385, ☎432 6461).

During the rest of the year the house is closed to the public, but in the winter season you can watch a game of polo on the grounds, normally on alternate Saturday afternoons.

## Bagatelle Great House

Daily 9am–5pm. Free. This is one of the best examples of early Barbadian vernacular architecture. A classic double staircase leads up to the old living quarters, fronted by a columned porch with a decorated pediment, while the entrance below the porch leads into deep cellars that once served as the house's food stores.

In keeping with tradition, the great house was named by a former owner who, having lost the estate in a dice game, derided it as "a mere bagatelle". Today the upstairs rooms hold occasional displays of local art.

## Earthworks Pottery

Mon–Fri 9am–5pm, Sat 9am–1pm. The factory and shops here are worth a short detour off the main highway – from Bagatelle Great House head north and then immediately east on wiggly minor roads and you'll see the pottery signposted. Set up in 1975 to support the island's declining pottery industry (based largely at Chalky Mount, see p.107) the place has developed a great following among Bajans and tourists alike. This is a good source of colourful souvenirs: there are ranks of mugs, jugs, plates and vases for sale, and you can watch the potters at work.

## Sandy Lane

In Barbados, the name Sandy Lane is synonymous with the grandest of the island's hotels – a byword for Caribbean affluence and ostentation, with a list of repeat celebrity guests as long as your arm. Built in the early 1960s by Anglo–American Ronald Tree, a former parliamentary adviser to the government of Sir Winston Churchill, the hotel was designed to provide a winter retreat for the British upper classes, and the surrounding land was bought up for private homes for Tree's friends. These days, the likes of Mick Jagger and Michael Caine are regular winter visitors, but the place guards its guests jealously behind high walls and security guards.

Nevertheless, as part of his deal with the government to get permission for the hotel (and the re-routing of the coastal road that it involved), Tree promised to provide a ten-metre right of way to the south of the property, giving public access to the shore. Take advantage of that if you've got the energy and wander down to the bay past the tall casuarinas and manchineel trees. The sweep of gently shelving sand, backed by the elegant hotel (completely rebuilt between 1998 and 2001), is quite magnificent.

For details on the hotel's golf course, see p.139.

## Holetown

It was in present-day Holetown that English sailors first landed in Barbados in 1625, claiming the island for their king, James I, and naming the area St James' Town before moving on. Two years later the *William and John* landed at the same spot carrying a party of settlers; they renamed the place Holetown because an inlet from the sea – where they could anchor their shallow-draft ships – reminded them of the

▲ HOLETOWN RIVER

▲ ST JAMES FORT, HOLETOWN

Hole on the River Thames in London. The place developed slowly, quickly losing favour to the site of present-day Bridgetown, whose natural harbours offered better protection for shipping. Today, Holetown is a busy, modern hub for the local tourist industry, if somewhat lacking in character. All west coast buses run through the town, and the main highway is lined with fast-food restaurants, souvenir shops, banks and grocery stores.

## Sunset Crest, Chattel House Village and the West Coast Mall

Just before you reach the centre of Holetown, Sunset Crest, on the east side of the highway, has plenty of souvenir shops selling T-shirts, books and liquor, as well as guys selling fresh **coconut water** from a stand by the roadside. There are more shopping options in Holetown itself, where a dozen reproduction chattel houses alongside the highway sell gifts and souvenirs, and the nearby West Coast Mall offers equally good spending opportunities.

## James Fort and the Hole

West of the highway that runs through Holetown are a couple of places where you can cut down to the beach, though the sand is often crowded and narrow here and you're better off heading out of town if you want to swim. On the same side, the police station is built on the site of the old James Fort, a few of whose iron cannons still sit outside, next to an obelisk erected in 1905 to commemorate the 300th anniversary of the arrival of the first settlers. Though the historians of the time turned out to be several decades out with their calculations, this didn't stop them from enjoying a huge celebratory street party. An unapologetic corrective plaque was quietly fixed to the bottom of the obelisk in 1977 to mark the 350th anniversary of the first settlement.

A few minutes' walk north of here, 1st and 2nd Streets, lined with trendy restaurants, lead down to the sea. Further on, the scenery becomes more bucolic, with fields, cows and a cricket pitch by the roadside; a road

## The story of sugar

Commercial **sugar production** started in Barbados in 1643, using plants intro-
duced from Brazil by Dutch traders, and heralded a dramatic change in the
island's fortunes. The original dense forest that covered the island was chopped
down to leave bare land suitable for the new plantations, and the frontier farming
communities of European migrants were replaced by a slave-based plantation
society as Africans were brought in to labour in the sugar fields.

Barbados was England's first sugar-producing colony, and it provided fabulous
returns for plantation owners for well over a century. Though the island gradually
lost ground to the nearby production centre of Jamaica, tax and trade incentives
meant that growing sugar remained lucrative, and the planters celebrated their
wealth by building the lavish great houses that still overlook the cane fields from
breezy hilltop perches. However, the industry took two big hits in the mid-nine-
teenth century when the abolition of the slave trade in 1834 was followed by the
British Sugar Equalization Act of 1846, which ended preferential treatment for
sugar produced in the colonies.

Though no longer able to compete effectively with cheaper sugar from Cuba and
Brazil, the Barbadian sugar industry rumbled on into the twentieth century. Over
recent decades, attempts to save the industry have included centralization of factories and the introduction of modern mechanization. Though the windmills are no
longer turning, the swaying fields of cane that still dominate the island remain testament to the continuing importance of King Sugar.

bridge runs over the Hole,
which is alive with egrets
towards sunset.

### St James's Parish Church

Daily 9am–5pm. Free. St James's
Parish Church is one of the most
attractive of its kind on the
island, and also the oldest
religious site in Barbados – the
original wooden church was
built here in 1628. This was
replaced by a stone structure in
1660 but, as happened
throughout the island, hurricane
and fire damage took their toll,
and most of the present building,
including the elegant round
tower above the altar, dates from
between 1789 and 1874, when
the nave was extended. However,
there are older relics: the stone
pillars at the entrance to the
south porch are thought to date
from the seventeenth century,
while the baptismal font and the
iron bell in the north porch bear
the dates 1684 and 1696,
respectively.

The present church is a small
but graceful building, with thick
stone walls, and two columns
supporting the stone chancel
arch that divides the nave from
the choir. There are the usual
marble funerary monuments on
the walls, while more modern
works of art include a colourful
biblical triptych by Ethiopian
painter Alemayehu Bizumeh and
bronze bas-reliefs of St James
and St Mary by Czech sculptor
George Kveton. There are also
extracts from the church's old
register of births and deaths,
which records the short lives of
the early settlers, and a letter
from the White House
expressing Ronald and Nancy
Reagan's appreciation of a
service they attended here in
1982. Reagan's currying of
favour with Caribbean leaders
paid dividends a year later when
the majority – headed by
Barbados's Tom Adams – gave
avid support to the US invasion
of Grenada.

## Folkestone Marine Park

Mon–Fri 9am–4pm. B$1. Established in 1979, the Folkestone Marine Park extends down the coast as far as Sandy Lane Bay. For **snorkellers** there are some decent patches of coral reef just offshore; alternatively you can usually find a glass-bottomed boat to take you out and hunt for colourful fish and the occasional turtle. The visitor centre has a short video and a handful of reasonable displays on the island's coral reefs and other marine life. If you're just into loafing around, the beach outside the centre – a decent if narrow and rather rocky patch, backed by casuarina and manchineel trees – is popular with local families on weekends and holidays, and has a lifeguard, showers, snack bars and a sprinkling of beach vendors.

## Sir Frank Hutson Sugar Museum

Mon–Sat 9am–5pm. B$15. This small but informative museum offers a clear introduction to the product on which Barbados depended for nearly three hundred years. Housed in the former boiling house of the local Blowers sugar estate, which was built in the 1880s, the museum showcases a series of "tayches" or boiling pans in which the cane juice was heated, the scum or waste floating to the top and being ladled off before the residue was passed into the next, smaller pan en route to being turned into crystals. Elsewhere, there are giant pieces of mill machinery, as well as the tools of the blacksmiths and coopers who helped to keep the sugar estates running smoothly, but it is the old black and white photos that best evoke the era in which sugar was king – workers slaving in the fields, grinding the cane and racing the barrels of sugar through the streets of Bridgetown to catch the next boat to England.

Between February and June, the entrance price includes a tour of the adjacent sugar factory – a heady experience for the smell alone – where you can view the full production process, from the loading and grinding of the cane to the crystallization of the brown sugar, which is sent off for refining abroad. The factory was

▲ SPEIGHTSTOWN ESPLANADE

built in 1984 and, during its relatively short operating season, takes cane from 33 local plantations and more than six hundred small farmers.

## North to Mullins Bay

Beyond Folkestone, the highway heads north without too much of particular interest to hold you until Speightstown further north. A series of exclusive hotels and grand private houses, fenced in behind security gates, is interspersed with small villages of shops, fishing shacks and chattel houses, keeping a typically Bajan toehold on the increasingly developed west coast. Access from the main road to many of the small bays along the coast is difficult, but good snorkelling can be found offshore beside the *Lone Star* motel (endangered hawksbill **turtles** can also often be spotted here – look out for the buoys about 200m offshore, where you'll likely find one or two boats moored and snorkellers swimming with the turtles).

Unlike the hard to reach bays to the south, Mullins Bay – a strip of sugary sand with a lively beach bar – is a good place to stop for a swim. Buses stop here and there's a car park across from the bay next to the Suga Suga Spa. If it's crowded, wander off down the beach to find your own private spot.

Just before Mullins Bay, a signposted turn-off to the right leads up to the **Shell Gallery** (Mon–Fri 9.30am–4pm), a delightful little store selling a fantastic collection of shells, both individually and set in clusters. It's worth a look even if you've no interest in buying.

Just north of Mullins Bay turtles can be seen offshore from the *Cobblers Cove Hotel* – look out for other snorkellers and boats tied up nearby.

## Speightstown

Small, run-down and utterly charming, Speightstown (pronounced "Spikestown") is the second town of Barbados, though it remains largely untouched by tourist development. It was once a thriving port, famous for its tough-talking, uncompromising inhabitants – "Speightstown flattery" is an old Bajan term for a back-handed compliment. Over the last century, however, the place has declined precipitately; the old buildings were left to decay and a great fire in 1941 destroyed many historic quarters. Recent years have seen serious effort to preserve and re-create Speightstown's historic character, turning it into a "model town", but it remains an earthy, beguiling place, with old-fashioned Georgian-style shops fronting onto narrow streets, their galleries – propped up on wooden pillars – projecting out over the pavements. There is little to do

▲ FISH MARKET, SPEIGHTSTOWN

▲ FISHING BOAT, SIX MEN'S BAY

here but stroll around the remnants of the local fishing industry and a few stylish old buildings or dine at one of a handful of excellent restaurants.

Buses running up the west coast normally terminate at Speightstown, stopping at the eastern end of Church Street – from here, head down towards the sea and you'll pass the parish church on your right. Queen Street has an unofficial tourist information office in the *Fisherman's Pub* (see p.98).

## St Peter's Parish Church

Church Street, Speightstown. Daily 9am–5pm. Across from the Speightstown's Esplanade, this church was first built in the 1630s, making it one of the oldest churches in Barbados. Destroyed by the 1831 hurricane, the Georgian building was rebuilt in a graceful Greek Revival style – though with the standard tower tacked on for good measure – and the present incarnation was superbly restored after the place was gutted by fire in 1980. Its an airy, peaceful place as you'd expect, though there's nothing particular to catch the eye.

## Queen Street

Speightstown's main drag has several grand old buildings that have just about survived the town's decline. Opposite *Mango's* restaurant, **Arlington**, almost medieval in design, is a classic example of the island's early townhouses – narrow, tall and gabled, with a sharply sloping roof. The iron gateway and outside veranda were common features among the houses of the wealthy Speightstown merchants; this one probably belonged to a ship's chandler, with its shop downstairs and the family home on the two floors above. Arlington has been glamorously renovated – part of a general scheme for the revamping of Speightstown – and is worth a look for a glimpse of old Barbados.

While you're here, cross the road and check out the **Gallery of Caribbean Art** (Mon–Fri 9.30am–4.30pm) above the bank, where there are three rooms of paintings, sculptures and metalwork for sale by artists from Barbados and the wider Caribbean.

Two hundred and fifty metres past the north end of the town, in a bright yellow house with a veranda overlooking the beach, the **art gallery** of the self-styled Gang of Four (Mon–Fri 10am–4pm) is worth a look for the local paintings of Gordon Webster, Sarah Venables and Azziza, and the sculpture of Ras Bongo Congo.

### Six Men's Bay

Heading north, the main road passes the spectacular Port St Charles marina, where luxury apartments with their own yachting berths change hands for millions of dollars. Beyond here starts a series of small, quiet fishing villages; perhaps the most picturesque of these is the former whaling port of Six Men's Bay, where brightly painted fishing boats line the shore.

### Maycock's Bay

This lovely area is the site of Maycock's Fort, one of the island's principal defences in the seventeenth century. It was built in 1638, just north of a small river inlet, to protect against enemy incursion, though sadly, the fort's ancient coral stone walls and powder magazines are now almost completely ruined, and few people make the effort to reach it. It's just a short stroll down from the end of the paved track.

## Accommodation

### Almond Beach Village

Heywoods ☎422 4900, ☏422 0617, ⍟www.almondresorts.com. By far the largest hotel on the island, this popular all-inclusive spreads along a lengthy stretch of beach just north of Speightstown. Besides numerous bars, restaurants and activities, there are nine pools, a small golf course, a nursery and a kids' club, and if you get bored of the beach you can try out their cookery or dancing classes. All-inclusive rates from US$125 per day.

### Angler Apartments

Derricks ☎ and ☏432 0817, ⍟barbadosahoy.com/angler. A dozen good-value, self-catering apartments in three small blocks shaded by mango and breadfruit trees and set back 200m from the highway just south of the *Coconut Creek Hotel*. The fan-

▲ MAYCOCK'S FORT

▲ CRYSTAL COVE, APPLEBY

spacious rooms are cleverly hidden around a large, beautiful garden. The main building – bright pink in colour but very English country house in design and furnishing – holds a splendid bar and restaurant (as well as two spectacular suites) and fronts onto a pleasant and relatively empty beach. Overall, one of the most delightful hotels on the island. Rooms from US$590/340 in winter/summer.

### Crystal Cove

Appleby ☎ 424 2683, ⓦ www.crystalcove hotelbarbados.com. One of the best of the island's all-inclusive hotels, with comfortable rooms, excellent food, good water sports and several pools (one with a swim-up bar under a waterfall). It's one of four west coast hotels owned by Elegant Hotels (all connected by a free boat taxi), and you're welcome to use the facilities at the sister hotels (pay a supplement for dinner at those which aren't all-inclusive). All inclusive rates from around US$175 per person.

### Escape

Prospect ☎ & ⓕ 424 7571. Unpretentious all-inclusive warmly decked out in bright, pastel colours and popular with tour groups. Water sports are limited – no waverunners or waterskiing – but the beach is great and the food is pretty good too. Ask for an ocean-view room on the second floor. Rates from $275/210 in winter/summer.

cooled rooms are comfortable, the atmosphere relaxed and friendly (the charming owners live on the premises), and you're just five minutes' walk from a good beach. Rooms from US$90/60 in winter/summer.

### Beachcomber Apartments

Paynes Bay ☎ 432 0489, ⓕ 432 2824, ⓦ www.beachcombersuites.com. Small apartment block that's popular with families, offering large, luxurious, air-conditioned two-bedroom apartments – each with a huge balcony overlooking Paynes Bay – sleeping up to six, and studios with smaller balconies sleeping two. The larger rooms have full kitchens; the studios small kitchenettes. Rooms from US$100/70 in winter/summer.

### Cobblers Cove Hotel

Between Speightstown and Mullins Bay ☎ 422 2291, ⓕ 422 1460, ⓦ www.cobblerscove.com. Forty

### King's Beach Hotel

Near Speightsown ☎ 422 1690, ☏ 422 1691. Large, spacious place, popular with German and Dutch package tourists, though it could do with a fresh lick of paint. The beach here is gorgeous and there's an extensive array of free water sports to try out if you can ever get past the pool. Rooms from US$180/100 in winter/summer.

### Little Good Harbour

Shermans ☎ 439 3000, ☏ 439 2020, ⓦ www.littlegoodharbourbarbados.com. New and friendly little hotel in a quiet spot north of Speightstown, more reasonable than some of the outrageously priced west coast places, with one- and two-bedroom suites in wooden gingerbread cottages, complete with kitchens, balconies and four-poster beds. There's a good restaurant next door. Rooms from US$302/226 in winter/summer.

### Lone Star

Mount Standfast ☎ 422 1617, ☏ 419 0597, ⓦ www.thelonestar.com. Fabulous, ultra-trendy and highly recommended little boutique hotel with four spectacular suites right over the beach. The massive rooms feature walk-in showers and stylish furniture, and each has a veranda where you'll be served breakfast as you look over the palm trees and out to sea. Also home to one of the island's trendiest restaurants (see p.99). Rooms from US$600/350 in winter/summer.

### Mango Lane Apartments

Speightstown ☎ 422 3146. An assortment of colourful and lightly furnished chattel houses and apartments dotted around the local area, rented out by the friendly owners of the *Fishermen's Pub* in Speightstown from US$40 per night.

### Sandridge Beach Hotel

Near Speightstown ☎ 422 2361, ☏ 422 1965. Three-storey hotel on a lovely strip of beach edged with tall coconut palms, and as good value as you'll find on the west coast. It's not fancy, but the rooms are sizeable and brightly decorated. There are two restaurants and a large pool, and great snorkelling just offshore. Very popular with families.

▲ SANDY LANE HOTEL, SANDY LANE

Rooms from US$110/90 in winter/summer.

## Sandy Lane

☎ 432 1311, ℻ 432 2954, ⓦ www.sandylane.com. The jewel of the west coast, a magnificent place in every way, offering spectacular luxury in the rooms, restaurants, bars and other communal areas. If you need to ask the price you can't afford it. Room from US$700/450 in winter/summer.

## Settlers Beach

Settlers Beach ☎ 432 0840, ℻ 432 2147, ⓦ www.settlersbeachhotel.com. Delightful apartment hotel on a great stretch of beach, attractively landscaped and with a fine freshwater swimming pool. The large rooms (from US$222/109 in winter/summer) make it a good choice for families.

## Smugglers' Cove

Paynes Bay ☎ 432 1741, ℻ 432 1749, ⓦ www.barbados.org./hotels/smugglerscove. Small, friendly but slightly cramped hotel complete with gardens filled with crotons. The 21 rooms (from US$140/74 in winter/summer) all have tiny kitchenettes, and there's a bar-restaurant and a small swimming pool just 10m from the beach. A decent value considering its expensive west coast location, particularly during the summer.

## Sunset Crest

Sunset Crest ☎ 432 6750, ℻ 432 7229, ⓦ www.sunsetcrestbarbados.com. Large, sprawling resort ten minutes' walk from the beach, with several swimming pools, restaurants and bars, and over a hundred one-, two- and three-bedroom apartments scattered around the complex. Rates for the rather tatty smaller rooms start at US$95/65 in winter/summer (US$495/325 per week), though it's worth paying a few dollars extra for the more secluded apartments. Two-bedroom villas rent for US$120/85, with a $10 per person surcharge if there are more than two of you.

## Treasure Beach

Paynes Bay ☎ 432 1346, ℻ 432 1094, ⓦ www.barbados.org./hotels/h64.htm. Small, unpretentious and charming hotel, with thirty large one-bedroom suites arranged around a small pool (from US$485/195 in winter/summer). The comfortable rooms include kitchenettes and sofa beds, though no televisions or radios to shatter the peace. The hotel restaurant is first-rate and the place boasts some of the friendliest staff around.

# Restaurants

## Angry Annie's

1st Street, Holetown ☎ 432 2119. Mon–Sat 6–10pm. Brightly painted building (and equally bright inside) just off the main highway, with a decent selection of local food – starters of fisherman's soup or flying fish fillets for around B$13, main courses of multicoloured Rasta pasta for B$30, chicken curry for B$40 or limbo lamb for B$55.

## Back to Eden

Jordan's Plaza, Queen Street, Speightstown. Mon–Fri 10am–4pm. One of very few vegetarian places on Barbados, serving tasty island stews and other dishes.

Changing daily juices like carambola or golden plum are worth dropping in for, as are the oat, honey and banana shakes and freshly baked cakes.

## Café Flindt

1st Street, Holetown ☎ 432 2626. Mon–Fri 7am–5pm; Sat & Sun 7am–noon. Upmarket bakery/patisserie selling home-made breads and sandwiches and mouthwatering cakes and pastries. Eat in or take out.

## Carambola

Prospect ☎ 432 0832. Mon–Sat 6.30–10.30pm. Tasty Caribbean food served in a lovely outdoor setting on a cliff overlooking the ocean. Starters, such as poached chicken livers, tuna sashimi and grilled squid with tomato and onion salsa cost B$22–30. Main courses include wine-poached mahi-mahi, oven roasted duck with aniseed marmalade, spiced chicken in mango sauce and fresh pasta dishes (B$42–66).

## The Cliff

Fitts ☎ 432 1922. Daily 6–10.30pm. This longstanding west coast favourite is located in a beautiful, pillared coral stone building on a cliff-top, complete with a small army of waiters, flaming torches and exquisite food. Expect some of the island's most innovative cooking – and to pay B$140 for two courses before drinks.

## Daphne's

Paynes Bay ☎ 432 2731. Daily 6.30–10.30pm and (in high season) 12.30–3pm. Elegant waterside restaurant turning out delicious Italian–Caribbean fusion food. Try interesting starters like endive, pear and pecorino salad

or San Daniele ham with zucchini and Montasio cheese, (B$19–35), and main courses such as calves' liver with sage mash or pork saltimbocca (B$50–60). Pasta dishes, including linguine with spicy crab or potato gnocchi, run to B$40–50.

## Emerald Palm

Porters ☎ 422 4116. Daily 6–10.30pm. Elegant place with ten tables on a patio beside a beautifully landscaped garden. The service is welcoming and the food is top-class: starters of Thai fish cakes or grilled squid (B$15–30), main courses of rack of lamb in a mustard and herb crust and deliciously fresh catch of the day (B$45–60).

## Fish Pot

Little Good Harbour ☎ 439-2604. Daily 11am–3pm and 6–10pm. A perfect setting – a coral stone house with ocean views – showcasing good food from an ambitious and unusual menu: cardamom-roasted kangaroo rump, steamed clams and fried *goujon* of alligator starters for B$28–35, main courses of lamb shanks, pan-fried barracuda or sauteed shrimp for B$45–55.

## Fisherman's Pub

Queen Street, Speightstown ☎ 422 2703. Daily 11am–10pm, live music 6–11pm. Delightful place, with a large veranda jutting out over the ocean and the best-value food in town. You can munch on a sizeable roti or flying fish cutters at lunch for around B$5; at night, typical Bajan dinners cost around B$20. Usually the liveliest place in town, with a steel band on Wednesday nights, and occasional floor shows on the ocean-front veranda.

▲ MANGO'S, SPEIGHTSTOWN

## Garden Bar

*Angler Apartments,* Derricks ☎432 0817. Daily 6–8.30pm. Small, laid-back, no-frills place offering traditional West Indian meals like pepperpot, cook-up rice (rice and peas with salt beef and lamb, cooked in coconut milk) and, occasionally, Guyanese specialities like *metagee* (a root vegetable stew of plantains), cassava, eddoes and dumplings served with shredded beef or fish. Reckon on spending $25–30 per person. Worth calling ahead, as some of the specialities take a while to prepare.

## La Mer

Port St Charles ☎419 2000. Tues–Sat 7–9.30pm, Tues–Fri 12.30–3.30pm, Sun 12.30–2pm. Top chef Hans Schweitzer has garnered plenty of plaudits for imaginative cook-ing and top-notch ingredients (try the stir-fried fish and shell-fish in an oyster ginger broth). Sunday brunch here is a west coast ritual.

## La Terra

*Royal Westmoreland* resort, Holetown ☎432 1099. Mon–Sat 11.30am–10pm. Some of the best food on the island. Choose from starters like sesame seared tuna carpaccio or fresh asparagus with Parma ham (B\$20–30) and main courses of pan-fried barracuda in Cajun spices or fresh dolphinfish curry (B\$45–75).

## Lone Star

Mount Standfast ☎419 0598. Daily 11.30am–10.30pm. One of the trendiest of the west coast dining spots, in a relaxed but spectacular location by the sea. Expect to see fish soup, sushi or delicious tuna tartare as starters (B\$25–50), along with a variety of caviar or Alaskan crab legs for the self-indulgent. Main courses range from piri piri shrimp or jerk chicken to seared tuna or pork tenderloin in a cider sauce (B\$50–75). Overall, a restaurant that's worth going out of your way for.

## Mango's

Speightstown ☎422 0704. Daily 6–10pm. Classy favourite by the ocean offering friendly service and spectacular local cooking. The extensive menu features starters like an incredible crab spring roll, lobster bisque or blackened shrimp for B\$18–25, and main courses of fresh fish, ribs and filet mignon for B\$42–65. The passion-fruit cheesecake (B\$18) is a sensation-al way to finish.

### The Mews

2nd Street, Holetown ☎ 432 1122. Daily 5.30–11pm. Top-notch food is served at this Holetown townhouse – ask for a table on one of the upstairs terraces. The seafood is imaginative – try fresh dolphin fish in a parmesan crust, or lightly seared yellow fin tuna with coriander cream – and the place is often packed with local bigwigs. Reckon on B$20–30 for starters, B$50–70 for main courses.

### Olive's Bar & Bistro

2nd Street, Holetown ☎ 432 2112. Daily 6–10pm. Popular Holetown eatery, simple in design with its wooden floor and white tablecloths, but offering a wide choice of excellent meals. Regular starters include carpaccio of tuna with a cucumber salsa or warm shrimp salad (B$25–30), with main courses of fettucini with tomato and basil sauce, pan-fried calamari in garlic, chilli and lime, or blackened grouper (B$30–56). The upstairs bar is one of the best places to hang out for an early evening drink or a late-night chill.

### Ragamuffins

1st Street, Holetown ☎ 432 8000. Daily 11am–2.30pm & 6–10pm. Colourful and longstanding chattel house restaurant serving reliable and sensibly priced Caribbean food in an unpretentious atmosphere. Starters run from B$13 to B$21, while main courses such as blackened shrimp, seafood curry or jerk chicken will set you back between B$38 and B$46.

### Tam's Wok

1st Street, Holetown ☎ 432 8000. Daily 11am–2.30pm & 6–10pm. The best Chinese food in the Holetown area, with a lively host and a familiar menu that includes excellent sweet and sour dishes from B$26, chow meins for B$20 and plenty of good vegetarian and seafood options.

## Bars

### Bombas

Prospect ☎ 432 0569. Daily 11am–10pm in winter, 11am–6pm in summer. Casual and fun beach bar under the trees offering inexpensive roti, chicken and fish snacks during the day and changing daily pasta, curry and vegetarian specials for B$30–40 in the evening.

### Chattel House

*Sandridge Beach Hotel*, near Speightstown. Daily 11am–9pm. Slightly sanitized but hugely engaging version of a typical Bajan rum shop, brightly painted and with traditional wooden furniture and enthusiastic service. The menu features good inexpensive cutters, burgers, pies and chicken, and if you're around on a Saturday, don't miss the weekend special of **pudding and souse** – an absolute steal at B$10.

### Coach House

Paynes Bay ☎ 432 1163. Daily noon–3pm and 6–10.30pm, live music 8pm–2am. This bustling place re-creates the style of a traditional English pub, with indoor and outdoor bars. It's often a good place to catch live bands and to see English and American sport beamed in by satellite. The food is fine but nothing to write home about – barbecued chicken, jerk pork, beef in beer or fresh dolphin for around B$30–40, and a curry night on Fridays for B$25.

## Crocodile's Den

Paynes Bay ☎ 432 7625. Daily from
4pm, live music 8pm–3am. Funky
cocktail bar with pool tables,
darts and a great late-night
atmosphere. Usually features live
music on Fridays and Saturdays,
with local bands and DJs, and
occasional Latin nights when
you'll be obliged to learn to
dance the salsa along with
everyone else.

## Marshalls

Holders Hill, opposite the playing field.
Daily noon–2pm & 5–9pm.
Easygoing local bar serving a
wide selection of single dishes
for around B$15 – try the
curried chicken, flying fish or
stewed beef, all served with rice
and peas, macaroni pie and salad.
   Though 1.5km inland, this is
an essential stop for cricket fans
– the owner is cricket-mad, the
walls are papered with cricketing
memorabilia and former players
are regular guests.

## Suga Suga Beach Bar

Mullins Beach ☎ 422 1878. Mon–Sat
8.30am–10.30pm, Sun 8.30am–7pm.
One of the busiest bars on the
west coast, with good if rather
pricey all-day dining at tables on
a wide ocean-view veranda. The
Bajan fish soup and conch salads
(B$25–35) are excellent, as are
the grilled steaks, pigs' tails and
fried pork chops (B$30
upwards).

## Surfside Beach Bar

Behind the police station, Holetown
☎ 432 2105. Daily 9am–midnight. A
buzzing beach bar that's popular
from morning to night, with
lunches of sandwiches
(B$10–12), pasta or fish and
chips (B$20) and dinner options
like lasagne, fresh fish or a
seafood platter (B$27–35).
There's a daily happy hour
4.30–5.30pm, sports on satellite
TV and steel pan music on
Sunday evenings.

# Central Barbados

The landscape of the quiet central parishes of St George and St Thomas is almost uniformly flat or gently rolling – perfect for the sugar crop that's been under cultivation here for almost four centuries. North of here towards the parish of St Andrew, however, the land rises in a short series of peaks to the island's highest point, Mount Hillaby.

Despite its small area, **central Barbados** offers a variety of attractions to lure you away from the beach, including a couple that offer a unique glimpse of the island in its primal state: Welchman Hall Gully and the virgin forest at **Turner's Hall Woods**, little disturbed since the island was first visited by Europeans. There are negligible facilities here, though, and nowhere to really base yourself.

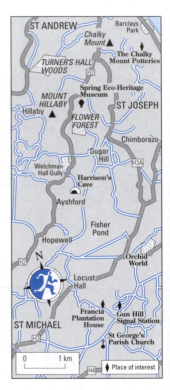

### St George's Parish Church

Daily 9am–4pm. Free. This parish church was originally built in the 1630s, a decade after the British first settled in Barbados, but like all of the island's old wooden churches, it was destroyed in the ferocious hurricane of 1780. The present building dates from 1784, and is the oldest complete church in the

(see p.129 for a list of rental agencies).

## Getting there and getting around

Getting to and around the interior of Barbados is straightforward – **buses** from Bridgetown run to the main attractions, though services are less frequent than on the coasts. You'll save a lot of time (and do a lot more exploring) if you rent a car for a day or two – a network of country lanes crisscross the centre, offering easy access from the coast (see p.129 for a list of rental agencies).

## Signal stations

Gun Hill was one of a chain of six **signal stations** that were quickly constructed on high ground across Barbados after the island's first and only mass slave revolt in 1816. In the era before the telephone, semaphore flags and lanterns were the fastest means of communication over long distances. The stations could rapidly pass signals between the east and west coasts; within minutes of trouble in even the remotest part of the island, the garrison in Bridgetown could be put on alert, or have soldiers marching out to quell any trouble. The stations were also on standby to warn of the arrival of enemy ships, though in the event neither domestic revolt nor enemy invasion took place, and the semaphore signals were only ever used to advise of the safe arrival of cargo and passenger ships. With the introduction of the telephone, the stations became unnecessary and were abandoned in 1887. Two other signal stations survive on Barbados: the Cotton Tower in St Joseph (see p.119) and Grenade Hall in the north of the island (see p.110).

country. With its Georgian arched windows and doors, and Gothic buttressing and battlements, the church is an odd architectural hybrid. However, the altar painting of the resurrection, *Rise to Power,* by Benjamin West, is one of the best church paintings on the island, and elsewhere are several fine marble commemorative sculptures made in England, including a tablet by Richard Westmacott, sculptor of the statues of Nelson in Trafalgar Square, London and in Bridgetown. The airy chancel is notable for its attractive series of stained-glass windows illustrating biblical scenes. Outside, the extensive cemetery, where old tombs crumble beneath various types of palm, offers a shady stroll and lovely views.

### Gun Hill Signal Station

Mon–Sat 9am–5pm. B$10. Gun Hill Signal Station sits among pretty landscaped gardens that belie its turbulent origins. Built in 1818 and impressively restored by the Barbados National Trust, the watchtower offers fabulous panoramic views across the green, gently rolling hills of central Barbados and out to the

▲ LION STATUE AT GUN HILL

ocean beyond Bridgetown. Guides give an expert introduction to the local history, and there is a small but immaculate display of military memorabilia, including flags of the various army regiments that were stationed here, maps of the island's many forts – 23 of them had been built as early as 1728 – and the cannons (never fired) that would have alerted the population to enemy invasion. Below the station, and visible from the tower, is a giant white lion – a British military emblem carved from a single block of limestone by soldiers stationed here in 1868.

## Francia Plantation House

Mon–Fri 10am–4pm. B$10. A working plantation, Francia grows sweet potatoes, yams and eddoes (a type of yam) for export. The plantation house is one of the most attractive in Barbados; it was also one of the last of the island's great houses, built at the turn of the twentieth century when the plantations were in decline as the value of sugar fell on world markets. The sweeping front staircase, triple-arched entrance and enclosed upper balcony are unusual features, reflecting the tastes of the original French owner, while the huge terraced garden feels very English in style, despite the abundance of tropical flora, including a gigantic mammee apple tree, frangipani, hibiscus and the ubiquitous bougainvillea. Inside, a spectacular chandelier hangs over the dining table, and there's the usual array of mahogany furniture, much of it predating the house itself. What distinguishes Francia from the other great houses you can tour, however, is the superb collection of antique maps of Barbados and the Caribbean, collected from dusty bookshops and grand auction rooms around the world and dating back to the early sixteenth century, only decades after Columbus first "discovered" the region.

## Orchid World

Daily 9am–5pm. B$14.75. A stunning collection of around 20,000 orchids is displayed among the lovely coral rock gardens and orchid houses of Orchid World, one of the island's newer botanical

▲ FRANCIA PLANTATION HOUSE

▲ PALM FRONDS

attractions. Built on the site of an old chicken farm and surrounded by fields of sugar cane, it's a pretty place – including bougainvillea, ferns, palms and a waterfall – that will take you no more than a comfortable hour to wander around. Unless you're an orchid enthusiast, though, the Flower Forest (see p.106) and Andromeda Botanical Gardens (see p.120) offer rather more in the way of interest and diversity.

## Harrison's Cave

40min tours daily 9am–4pm. B$25.
Harrison's Cave is an enormous subterranean labyrinth, where underground streams and dripping water have carved huge limestone caverns filled with strangely shaped calcite formations. Visitors are taken underground and around the various chambers on an electric tram, which, with the guide's mechanical voice-over, rather spoils the eerie, otherwise soundless atmosphere of the place, though it doesn't completely detract from the beauty – you'll be hard put to find more spectacular cave scenery anywhere in the world. A twelve-metre waterfall plunges into one of the smaller caves; a river pours silently through another; while, in a third, a huge icy green lake offers a unusual swimming opportunity if you've

got the nerve. The guide points out some of the eye-catching shapes made by the dripping limestone: the pope, a mother and child, and a flock of vultures.

## Springvale Eco-Heritage Museum

Highway 2. Mon–Sat 10am–4pm. B$5.

This small folk museum offers a glimpse of some disappearing ways of Bajan life. Besides a collection of locally made furniture, there are traditional cooking pots and exhibits on the mining of manjak, known as "Barbados tar". Browse the extensive library extensive or take a pleasant stroll through the grounds, which used to be part of a sugar plantation and now have a diverting nature trail that leads to an old manjak mine. The café serves cakes and soft drinks, including the traditional **mauby**, made from boiling up pieces of a bitter tree bark with spices like aniseed and cinnamon.

## Welchman Hall Gully

Mon–Sat 9am–5pm. B$11.50. The dramatic Welchman Hall Gully is a long, deep corridor of jungle, hemmed in by steep cliffs and abounding with local flora and fauna. Though a handful of non-indigenous plants have been planted here over the years, the vegetation is not dissimilar to that which covered the whole island when the British first arrived here. There are two entrances – one at either end of the gully – and buses from Bridgetown stop outside each one. A marked trail (1km) runs through the gully, past abundant fruit and spice trees dangling with lianas, such as clove and fig trees, as well as the numerous ginger lilies, ferns and palms. Keep an eye out for

▲ SUGARCANE FIELDS

green monkeys, which can be spotted in the undergrowth during the early morning or late afternoon.

## The Flower Forest

Signposted just south of Highway 2. Daily 9am–5pm. B$13.80. The immaculately landscaped Flower Forest boasts a great variety of indigenous and imported plants and trees, all labelled with their Latin and English names and country of origin, as well as some fabulous views over the hills of the Scotland district, but overall the place feels just a little bit too neat and ordered. If you only have time to visit one of the island's botanical gardens, you're probably better off making for the more rugged Andromeda Botanical Gardens on the east coast (see p.120), but the Flower Forest is certainly worth a look if you're in the area.

The garden, divided into sections coyly named "Don's Downhill", "Colin's Corner" and "Mary's Meadow", takes about half and hour to walk through by way of a path that runs around their borders. The

seemingly endless list of trees includes breadfruit, coffee, Barbados cherry, avocado and a single African baobab tree, and there is a fine collection of orchids, hibiscus and the "lobster claw" heliconias as well. Another highlight is the Palm Walk, where dozens of different types of palm are scattered around, making for a pleasant, shady place to cool off with a picnic and a good book.

## Mount Hillaby

Mount Hillaby, at 335m, is the highest point on Barbados, with suitably commanding views of the island. Make a left turn at the village of Baxters – a sharp uphill beside a faded pink chattel house – and follow the road straight through to the pretty little village of Hillaby. (The road maybe covered in markings for **road tennis** – a Bajan invention, formerly known as poor man's tennis and played with paddle bats and a tennis ball to table-tennis rules on a six-metre by three-metre court.) Turn left by the church, past the mini mart, and follow the road for over a kilometre to the very top, where you can park. From here, you can look out over the Atlantic-lashed east coast, or take the grassy and sometimes overgrown path on the right that leads to the summit and more panoramic views.

## Turner's Hall Woods

This is the last area of Barbados still covered in the primary rainforest that the first settlers encountered when they landed on the island. As soon as you set foot in the woods, which cover around fifty acres, the humidity makes you aware that you have entered a radically different ecosystem. Although there's no particular target to make for, you can follow the track (once a proper road) that leads through the centre of the woods. This is a fascinating and atmospheric place to wander, buzzing with bird life and surrounded by ancient vegetation – lianas, mahogany trees and some magnificent silk cotton trees.

To get to Turner's Hall, take the signposted left off Highway 2 to St Simons soon after you pass Haggatts government agriculture station. Follow the side road through the small rural village and right to the end of the track, where you can park a hundred metres from the entrance to the woods. If you're coming by bus, look for the St Simons or Shorey bus from Bridgetown.

## Chalky Mount

Signposted to the right off Highway 2. Chalky Mount is the highest peak on a range of hills famous for its reddish-brown clay. Potters have operated in the area for generations, and the small village of Chalky Mount – a short hike from the summit – still counts a handful among its residents, making and selling sensibly priced mugs, pots and "monkey jugs", traditionally used for keeping drinking water cool.

▲ HANDCRAFTED MUGS, CHALKY MOUNT

# The north

The **north** of Barbados is the most rugged and least visited part of the island, but nonetheless offers an excellent variety of places to explore. The most popular target is the Barbados Wildlife Reserve, home to hundreds of green monkeys and a host of other animals; nearby, there's an old signal station and a nature trail through the forest at Grenade Hall. Other specific attractions include a working sugar mill at Morgan Lewis and a superb Jacobean great house, St Nicholas Abbey, while the northerly parish of St Lucy offers some dramatic cliff-top scenery. There are no hotels or restaurants along this stretch of the north coast; the closest you'll find are over in Speightstown, on the west coast.

## Barbados Wildlife Reserve

Daily 10am–5pm. B\$23, including access to Grenade Hall. This wildlife reserve, just off Highway 1 and directly accessible by bus from Speightstown or Bridgetown, was originally established for the conservation of **green monkeys** and – more

▼ DEER, BARBADOS WILDLIFE RESERVE

controversially – to look at the possibility of exporting them for medical research, particularly in the production and testing of vaccines. As the idea of turning the reserve into a tourist attraction developed, other creatures were gradually introduced, including brocket deer, who normally hide in the undergrowth, otters, armadillos, racoons and caiman alligators, as well as caged parrots, macaws and other fabulously coloured tropical birds.

Paths meander through the lush mahogany woods here and, in a thirty-minute stroll, you'll see pretty much everything on offer – the aviary, fishponds, birdcages and plenty of animals. The monkeys are the highlight, swarming freely around the reserve, and you can sometimes

## Getting there and getting around

**Buses** run through the northern parishes from both Speightstown and Bridgetown, though services are less regular than along the south and west coasts. If you're planning to visit more than one of the main attractions – and you could comfortably see all of them in a day – renting a car will make getting around a lot less hassle.

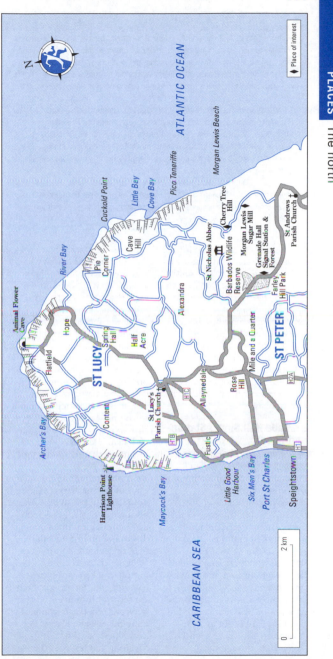

N

CARIBBEAN SEA

ATLANTIC OCEAN

Harrison Point Lighthouse

Animal Flower Cave

Archer's Bay

Maycock's Bay

Little Good Harbour

Six Men's Bay

Port St Charles

Speightstown

River Bay

Cuckold Point

Little Bay

Cove Bay

Pica Teneriffe

Morgan Lewis Beach

Flatfield

Hope

Content

St Lucy's Parish Church

Spring Hall

Half Acre

Pie Corner

Cave Hill

Alexandra

**ST LUCY**

Fustic

Alleynedale

Rose Hill

Mile and a Quarter

Barbados Wildlife Reserve

St Nicholas Abbey

Cherry Tree Hill

Morgan Lewis Sugar Mill

Grenade Hall Signal Station & Forest

Farley Hill Park

St Andrews Parish Church

**ST PETER**

H1C

H1B

H2A

H1

▶ Place of interest

0    2 km

## Green monkeys

**Green monkeys** first came to Barbados from West Africa around 1650, almost certainly as pets of the slave traders on one of the early ships. They soon established a firm footing in the island's woods and gullies and, though they haven't spread to the surrounding West Indies, they remain prolific on Barbados. They're shy creatures, but you've a good chance of seeing one (or even a troupe) of the estimated five thousand loping across a road as you drive around the interior.

Predictably, and to the fury of local farmers, the monkeys have a liking for many of the island's crops; as a result, a bounty has been offered on their heads (or tails) since 1679. Nowadays, the Primate Research Centre at the Barbados Wildlife Reserve offers a more substantial inducement if they are delivered alive, so you may see monkey traps scattered around – usually nothing more complex than a banana in a cage.

There is plenty of island folklore about the green monkeys, perhaps most endearingly that – like their human cousins – they bury their dead. Modern zoologists scoff at such suggestions but will, if pressed, admit that skeletons are rarely found.

see them making a break for the outside, leaping from trees over the perimeter fence; apparently, they always return. Don't try to get too close – they can inflict a nasty bite if provoked – and bear in mind that they are not averse to snatching cameras or bags left in an accessible place. Be sure to stop by the information centre, at the northeast corner of the reserve, which has excellent displays on the monkeys.

### Grenade Hall Signal Station and forest

Daily 10am–5pm. B$23, including access to Wildlife Reserve. The Grenade Hall Signal Station was one of the chain of communication stations (see box, p.103) built in the years immediately after Barbados faced its first and only major slave revolt in 1816. The stations, which communicated by semaphore flags and lanterns, were designed to get news of any trouble afoot rapidly to the garrison in Bridgetown. Grenade Hall is not as attractively located as Gun Hill (see p.102), though the

watchtower offers great views of the surrounding countryside, and the place is certainly worth a quick tour if you're in the area. Prints of the British military hang downstairs, alongside various bits and pieces belonging to the signalmen – medallions, clay pipes, coins and pottery shards, while upstairs some old semaphore signals are on display – though most of them post-date the era of possible slave revolts and relate to shipping movements. There is also an old-fashioned telephone and a small display on the invention that made the signal stations obsolete.

Below Grenade Hall is a large tract of **native forest** (same hours and ticket) where several kilometres of pathways loop down through whitewood, dogwood, mahogany and magnificent silk cotton trees. Walking down from the signal station you can feel yourself entering a different ecosystem – shaded and humid – and the network of paths is complex enough to make it easy to get lost (albeit briefly). Boards put up along the trails list the names and medicinal values of some of the plants and trees and, back at the entrance, there's a detailed description of traditional "bush medicine".

## Farley Hill National Park

Daily 8am–6pm. Free (cars B$3.50). This small, pleasant park sits at the top of a three-hundred-metre cliff with commanding views over the Scotland district. It's a good place to retreat with a picnic once you've finished looking around Grenade Hall. The park is the site of what was once a spectacular great house, built for a sugar baron in 1857 and opulently restored in 1956 when it was used as the setting for the movie *Island in the Sun*, starring Harry Belafonte. Hollywood descended in force, adding an immaculate new gallery, staircase and open veranda, painting the trees to get the "right" colour of leaf, and pumping colossal amounts of precious water into the leaky artificial lake. The movie was a reasonable success, but the place went up in flames a few years later, leaving the old house completely gutted. No attempt was made to repair the damage and in 1965 the government bought the land and converted it into a park. Today, the charred coral block walls of the rather ghostly mansion form the park's focus, surrounded by landscaped lawns and masses of fruit trees.

## Morgan Lewis Sugar Mill

Mon–Sat 9am–5pm. B$10. Set in the midst of the crumbling ruins of an old sugar factory – a tall chimney poking defiantly from the overgrown grass – Morgan Lewis Sugar Mill is the only windmill in Barbados that's still in operation. The island once boasted more than five hundred such mills, all grinding juice from the sugar cane that covered the island like a blanket, but mechanization has all but eliminated them from the countryside. The Morgan Lewis mill, if not an essential object of pilgrimage during your stay on Barbados, provides an attractive

▲ FARLEY HILL RUINS

and atmospheric glimpse of this part of the island's history.

Though it's no longer in commercial use, the mill – first built in the nineteenth century – is still in perfect working order. The sails, wheelhouse and British-made machinery have been thoroughly restored in recent years, and you'll get a demonstration of how the thick bamboo-like stems were pushed through mechanical grinders to extract cane juice to make sugar. There's also a small display on the history of the island's mills and a short video showing the Morgan Lewis mill operating.

### Morgan Lewis Beach

This is one of the most remote spots on the island and, given the strong undercurrents here, swimming is highly dangerous. To get here, head uphill from Morgan Lewis Sugar Mill, then turn onto a narrow road for a kilometre to the first houses of Boscobelle. Make a sharp right down a rutted but passable track that eventually leads to the grassy, windblown slopes above Morgan Lewis Beach. There's rarely anyone around this untamed area and no houses in sight, and it's a decent place to chill out for an hour or two before you continue touring.

### Cherry Tree Hill

Continuing north uphill, the main road sweeps past sugar fields before reaching a magnificent canopy of mahogany trees at Cherry Tree Hill. It's worth stopping to look behind you across the east coast and out to the Atlantic Ocean for one of the most spectacular views on the island. There is actually no record of cherry trees having existed here; the local legend that they were all chopped down because passers-by kept stealing the fruit sounds a little unlikely.

### St Nicholas Abbey

Mon–Fri 10am–3.30pm. B$10. St Nicholas Abbey is the oldest house on Barbados and one of only three Jacobean plantation houses left standing in all of the Americas (the others are the privately owned Drax Hall, also

▼ NORTH POINT

▲ VIEW UP CHERRY HILL

on Barbados, and a castle in Virginia, USA). Built during the 1650s, the white-painted house with its distinctive ogee gables was originally owned by two of the largest sugar-growers in the north of the island. The name St Nicholas, however, came about much later, on account of the house's early nineteenth-century owners who hailed from St Nicholas parish in Bristol, England. How the place came to be called an abbey, though, is unclear.

Included in the entrance fee is a rather lacklustre guided tour of the ground floor of the house (the upstairs is still used, and closed to visitors), which is crammed with eighteenth-century furniture, Wedgwood porcelain and other traditional accoutrements of the old Barbadian aristocracy. The outbuildings at the back of the house are rather more rustic, and include the original bathhouse and a four-seater toilet.

The tour of the house may be a little unexciting, but an evocative twenty-minute black and white film is shown on request, containing some great footage of the boats arriving at Bridgetown harbour and of the pre-war city, with its horse-drawn carts and early cars. Once you've seen the film, you can take a short stroll through the woods behind the house or grab a drink in the small café.

## Cove Bay

Head through Cave Hill to Pie Corner, where a signposted right turn takes you out to the bay. This is one of the most beautiful of a series of coves on the island's north coast. Although there's a small, stony beach here that you can clamber down to if you're desperate to swim, the water is rough and rocky and you'll probably want to wait until you're somewhere calmer. Much more appealing is the view – elegant rows of palm trees stand just above the water's edge, buffeted by the trade winds, and you can see down the entire length of the east coast. To the right, a white cliff rising up to a sharp point 76m above the sea is rather grandly known as Pico Tenerife.

Although a handful of local hustlers may offer to help you

find Cove Bay in return for an unspecified tip, you won't have any trouble finding it by on your own.

## Little Bay

Little Bay is a rocky, foam-sprayed spot where the surf has carved caves, tunnels and arches into the cliffs. Like elsewhere along the coast, it's not a great place to swim, but at low tide there are plenty of rockpools to explore and you can clamber out to look around the caves. Leatherback turtles occasionally crawl onto the beach here to bury their eggs, though your chances of seeing them or their trails are pretty remote.

## River Bay

This bay takes its name from a stream that runs out to the sea through a small, steep-sided valley. It's a popular weekend spot with Bajans, who drive down here for a picnic, and when the water is high it's a pleasant enough place to swim.

## Animal Flower Cave

☎439 8797 for information. Daily 10am–4pm. B$6. Right at the barren, rocky northern tip of the island, the rather spooky Animal Flower Cave has been a tourist attraction for centuries. Created by the battering of thousands of years of Atlantic waves, the cave is still out of bounds when the sea is rough, and you may want to call ahead if you're dubious about the weather. A guide takes visitors into the cave, clambering down some stairs and across a slippery floor overhung with stalactites and filled with sinkholes and rockpools, in which a handful of tiny but colourful sea anemones and filter-feeding tube worms (the "animal flowers") wave their little tentacles about. Early visitors like English clergyman Griffith Hughes collected the "flowers" in the 1740s, taking specimens home to supply mini-museums. Though the numbers of the "flowers" have been heavily depleted since Hughes's day, and do not live up to the advertising hype, the cave remains an eerie and evocative place.

## Archer's Bay

A rocky path west of Animal Flower Cave leads down to a small sandy beach at Archer's Bay – a popular local spot, signposted off the main highway, but often too rough for swimming. Heading south from here, the road leads down to the unremarkable and usually locked St Lucy's Parish Church.

# The east coast

**A handful of small but characterful places on the surf-lashed and little-touristed east coast offer a change from the built-up south and west of the island. Unless you're really looking to get away from it all, you probably won't want to spend your entire trip here, but it's a great, quiet spot to unwind for a couple of days, walking on the deserted beaches and escaping the crowds. If you can't spend a night or two in the area, do at least stop by one of the excellent restaurants around the laid-back old resort of Bathsheba for lunch.**

## Ragged Point

Highway 5 runs east across Barbados from Bridgetown, ending up at the easternmost end of the island near Ragged Point. Atlantic breakers pound the limestone cliffs here in one of the wildest and most isolated spots on Barbados. On a nearby peninsula stands the disused East Point Lighthouse, one of the main landmarks on this side of the island and a site providing dramatic views up the coast.

## Codrington College

Daily 10am–4pm. B$5. Just north of Consett Bay, on the cliff-top, are the handsome buildings of Codrington College. The place is named after Christopher Codrington – a wealthy Barbadian landowner and governor of the Leeward Islands from 1698 to 1702. The first degree-level institution in the English-speaking West Indies, it continues to teach theology to budding Anglican vicars, and is

▲ CODRINGTON COLLEGE

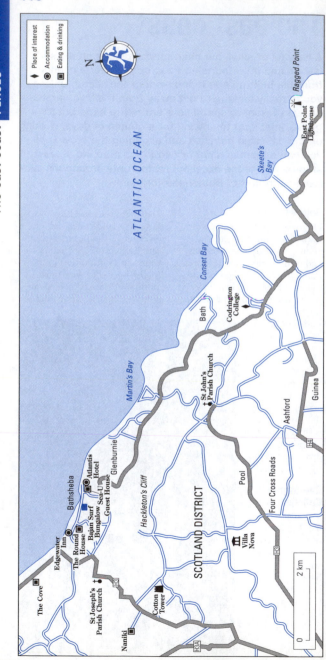

Place of interest
Accommodation
Eating & drinking

N

*Ragged Point*

East Point
Lighthouse

*Skeete's Bay*

ATLANTIC OCEAN

*Conset Bay*

Bath

Codrington
College

St John's
Parish Church

*Martin's Bay*

Atlantis
Hotel

Bathsheba

Bajan Surf
Bungalow Sea-U
Guest House

Glenburnie

Ashford

Guinea

*Hackleton's Cliff*

Pool

Four Cross Roads

Edgewater
Inn

The Round
House

SCOTLAND DISTRICT

Villa
Nova

The Cove

St Joseph's
Parish Church

Cotton
Tower

Namiki

0    2 km

▲ RAGGED POINT

now affiliated to the University of the West Indies.

The approach to the college is dramatic, along a long avenue lined on either side with a graceful row of tall cabbage palms and ending beside a large ornamental lake covered in waterlilies. The buildings are arranged around an unfinished quadrangle, with an arched central portico that opens onto large, elegant gardens offering panoramic views over the coast. The modest chapel is on your right as you enter, and the main hall, displaying a bust of Codrington, on your left. The principal's lodge, on the north side of the college, was the original seventeenth-century great house of the sugar plantation that once stood here and, though damaged by fire and hurricane, parts of the original structure still remain, including the coral stone porch and some of the carved Jacobean balustrades. A stone's throw to the west, a short nature trail has been laid out through the woods – a gentle place to wander for fifteen minutes or so.

## Bath

The tall, overgrown chimney of the ruined Bath sugar factory marks the turn-off to this curved brown sand beach. It's one of the safest places to swim on the east coast, backed by thick groves of casuarina trees and protected offshore by a long stretch of coral reef that makes the water here ideal for snorkelling. There's a children's play area, picnic tables by the water and, on weekends and holidays, a steady stream of Bajans coming to splash around and play beach cricket.

Back on the main road, you'll pass the giant satellite dish that keeps the island in touch with the outside world.

## Martin's Bay

The main road weaves in and out of the coast, past large sugar and banana plantations, en route to the small fishing village of Martin's Bay, which nestles on the coast beneath Hackleton's Cliff. The village makes a good starting point for a hiking tour of the coast. One appealing walk is between Martin's Bay

▲ SCOTLAND DISTRICT

and Bath, most of it following a trail along an old railway right-of-way, though at one point you'll have to cut inland around an abandoned railway bridge.

## St John's Parish Church

Daily 9am–5pm. Free. Like many of the parish churches, St John's – typically English with its arched doors and windows and graceful tower – was first built in the mid-seventeenth century but, following severe hurricane damage in the great storm of 1831, now dates from around 1836. The floor of the church is paved with ancient memorial tablets dating back as far as the 1660s, rescued from earlier versions of the building, and a Madonna and child sculpture by Richard Westmacott stands to the left of the main entrance. Most attractive of all is the reddish-brown pulpit, superbly hand-carved from four local woods (mahogany, ebony, manchineel and locust) and imported oak and pine. Outside, the expansive graveyard is perched on top of the cliff,

### Last of the Byzantines

One of the oldest tombs in the St John's graveyard is that of **Ferdinand Paleologus**, thought to have been the final surviving descendant of the brother of Constantine XI – the last emperor of the Byzantine Greeks – who was killed in battle when present-day Istanbul was captured by the Turks in 1453. Ferdinand's family moved to England, where he grew up, and he fought for King Charles I during the English Civil War. Like many defeated Royalists, he fled to Barbados in 1646, where he became a churchwarden of St John's and, later, a lieutenant in the militia.

Ferdinand's coffin was originally placed in a vault under the choir, facing in the opposite direction to the other coffins (with the head pointing west) and with the large skeleton embedded in quicklime, both customs of the Greek Orthodox Church. After the 1831 hurricane it was moved to the churchyard where it remains today. During the Greek War of Independence of the 1820s, the provisional Greek government made enquiries in Barbados to see if there was any surviving male descendant of Ferdinand still alive who might return as a figurehead for their new battle with the Turks. None was found.

looking down over miles of jagged coastline and crammed with moss-covered tombs, family vaults, a wide array of tropical flora.

## Hackleton's Cliff and Scotland

From St John's Parish Church, follow the road north where, after a kilometre or so, a sign diverts you right to Hackleton's Cliff. This steep 300m limestone escarpment marks the edge of the Scotland district to the west and, to the east, the rugged east coast whose limestone cap was eroded by sea action many centuries ago. At the end of a short track, you can park near the edge of the cliff for fabulous views across the craggy hills of Scotland, nostalgically named by early settlers for its supposed resemblance to the land of Robert Burns, and up the sandy northeast coastline. It's a peaceful spot, where the only sound is often the calling of the swifts as they wheel away on the warm currents of air rising from the ground hundreds of metres below.

## Villa Nova

North of the Hackleton's Cliff, a left-hand turn leads down to one of the most famous of the island's sugar plantation great houses. The new house ("villa nova") dates from 1833, after its predecessor was destroyed by the 1831 hurricane. Many of the island's leading dignitaries lived here, and former British prime minister Anthony Eden owned it for a while in the 1960s, entertaining Queen Elizabeth II here during her visit in 1966. Sadly, the cost of the upkeep defeated the last owners and the place has been converted into a luxury hotel (see p.122 for a review).

## The Cotton Tower

The main road runs through the tiny village of Easy Hall and continues past the derelict remains of Buckden Great House, overgrown and rather eerie with plants pushing their way up through the floorboards and green monkeys scampering around on the dilapidated roof. On the left, the pink Cotton Tower is one of the six signal stations built in the early nineteenth century to warn of slave uprisings or the arrival of enemy boats (see box, p.103). This particular one, built in 1819 and named for Lady Caroline Cotton, daughter of the island's governor, has been earmarked for renovation but is presently closed to visitors and rather run-down.

▼ COTTON TOWER

## Andromeda Botanical Gardens

**Daily 9am–5pm. B$15.** These colourful, sprawling gardens make up one of the most attractive spots on the island, spreading over a hillside strewn with coral boulders and offering fabulous vistas over the nearby coastline. Created by local botanist Iris Bannochie in 1954, the gardens feature masses of local and imported shrubs and plants landscaped around a trail that incorporates several ponds and a giant, ancient bearded fig tree.

The hibiscus garden, on your left as you enter, showcases every shade of hibiscus (even a grey hybrid), and is the best place to see the tiny hummingbirds that frequent the place. Trails take you around the gardens and past some old traveller's trees and a small clump of papyrus before turning uphill past a series of brilliant heliconia – including the bizarrely shaped "beefsteak" – and a panama hat tree. The bearded fig tree is the real star of the gardens, but there are plenty of other highlights, including a bank of frangipani, rose of Sharon trees, superb cycads and a *Bombax ellipticum*, also known as the shaving brush tree for the large pink-bristled flower it produces. At the lower end of the trail, the Queen Ingrid Palm Garden features dozens of types of palm, including the massive tailpot, largest of the fan palms and often used abroad for thatched roofing.

Local botanists offer an entertaining, free guided tour of the gardens each Wednesday at 10.30am.

The *Hibiscus Café*, inside the garden, serves cutters, rotis and other snacks as well as delicious Barbadian cherry juice, and there's a small gift shop selling prints, T-shirts, books and bottles of rum.

## Atlantis Hotel

Beyond the Andromeda Botanical Gardens the road continues down to the seafront and the *Atlantis Hotel*, a slightly faded and very easygoing place overlooking Tent Bay, which is often lined with the boats of the local fishing fleet. Built in the 1880s, this was one of the first hotels to be put up outside

▲ SHAVING BRUSH TREE

Bridgetown and, though there's not a great deal to do here, the place offers lunch and is a pleasant place to unwind with a drink or a stroll up the beach. For reviews of the lodging and restaurant see below and 122.

## Bathsheba

Picturesque, laid back and washed by Atlantic breezes, this has long been a favoured resort for Bajans, though surprisingly few tourists make it up here. Small holiday homes and the odd rum shop line the roadside as it runs along beside the sea.

If the bay here looks familiar, it's because this is one of the most painted landscapes in Barbados. Also known as the soup bowl, because of the crashing surf that comes racing in here pretty much all year round, the area is a popular surfing spot and the site of annual tournaments.

Unfortunately, the currents mean that it's not a good place to swim, but the wide brown beach here is attractive and there's an old pathway running north and south if you fancy a walk. Surfboards can be rented from a shack in the village (though it keeps rather irregular hours) or the far more reliable *Bajan Surf Bungalow* (see below).

For a pleasant hike, wander between Bathsheba and Cattlewash slightly to the north, along either the beach or the old railway track; en route, you'll cross Joe's River – one of just two permanently flowing rivers in Barbados – and can cut inland to look at the dense woods bordering it, before stopping for a bite to eat at one of the Bathsheba restaurants.

## Cattlewash and Shorey

Above Bathsheba, the east coast road runs alongside the eastern edge of the Scotland district through Cattlewash, a tiny village that derives its name from the traditional practice among local farmers of driving their cows down to the sea here. Continuing north, the road leads through Barclays Park, the small and wholly untouristed town of Belleplaine and the tiny village of Shorey, where the Conrad Hunte Sports Club (named for one of the greatest cricketers Barbados has produced) boasts perhaps the island's remotest cricket pitch, with the Atlantic Ocean glistening behind it.

# Accommodation

## Atlantis Hotel
Bathsheba ☎433 9445, ⊛www.atlantisbarbados.com. Ancient, faded and welcoming place overlooking picturesque Tent Bay, with great food that brings people from all round the island and eight modest rooms; ask for one with a balcony. Rooms from US$105/65 in winter/summer.

## Bajan Surf Bungalow
Bathsheba ☎433 9920, ⒻAX433 9278, ⊛www.bajansurfbungalow.com.
Small, friendly and utterly laidback place for (mainly) surfers to stay, with four private rooms and two dorm-style rooms that can each sleep up to five. Surf lessons and board hire are available. Rates from around US$25 per person.

## Edgewater Inn
Bathsheba ☎433 9900, ⒻAX433 9902, ⊛www.edgewaterinn.com. This local fixture, a once-attractive

but now rather run-down and forlorn place, is just above beautiful Bathsheba. Most of the rooms are ordinary, but a couple of them, 221 and 218, have balconies and sea views, and go for a higher rate (negotiable when things are quiet). There's a pool and hammocks, and a decent restaurant. Rooms from $130/102 in winter/summer.

### Round House Inn

Bathsheba ☎433 9678. More of a restaurant than a hotel – and the best place to eat on the east coast – but the owners rent out a few rooms upstairs (from US$100/75).

### Sea-U Guest House

Bathsheba ☎433 9450, ⓦwww.seaubarbados.com. Pleasant and friendly little German-managed guest house just above the *Atlantis Hotel*, surrounded by an acre of tropical garden. The rooms are comfortable and cosy and the atmosphere relaxed. Probably the best accommodation option on the east coast. Rooms from $95/65 in winter/summer.

### Villa Nova

Bathsheba ☎433 1524, ⓦwww.villanovabarbados.com. Luxurious former private mansion, now converted into an exclusive hotel, set back a short drive from the coast and a delightful place to escape the crowds. The accommodation and facilities are first rate. Rooms from US$700/$450 in winter/summer for bed and breakfast.

# Restaurants

### Atlantis Hotel

Bathsheba ☎433 9445. Daily noon–2.30pm & 5.30–7.30pm. Faded old hotel with loads of character and great home cooking. The vast Sunday buffet (B$45) is staggeringly good while the weekday prix fixe menu (B$33) includes a hearty soup, pork chops or fresh fish and a tasty dessert. The large number of locals who keep coming back is as good a recommendation as you'll get.

▲ BATH SUGAR FACTORY

## The Cove

Bathsheba ☎433 9495. Tues–Sun noon–3pm. Popular with Bajans and well worth stopping at if you're passing through. The friendly folk at *The Cove* offer tasty lunches that change daily but might include coconut chicken curry or fresh fish, as well as a range of soups and sandwiches. A filling lunch will set you back B$20–40.

## Naniki

Surinam ☎433 1300. Tues–Sun lunch noon–3.30pm; dinner during high season (call ahead). Delightful newcomer to the area serving innovative lunches (and dinners in season). Starters include grilled chicken salad with a curry and mango dressing (B$21), while mains might be grilled snapper (B$35), jerk chicken or pork with pineapple relish (B$37) or vegetarian options like stewed soya chunks with root vegetables or mock duck with lentils (B$28–32). Definitely worth a try.

## Round House Inn

Bathsheba ☎433 9678. Daily 11.30am–2.30pm & 6–10pm. Top-quality cooking and a casual, family atmosphere, halfway down the steep hill that plunges down to Bathsheba bay. The lunch and dinner menus are similar – with items like blackened catch of the day, shrimp scampi and home-made pasta specials for B$35–40 – but you can also get sandwiches and salads at lunchtime. There's an ocean view and you can sit indoors or on the veranda. Pretty much the only place for regular live music in the area, with a decent jazz or reggae band on several nights a week.

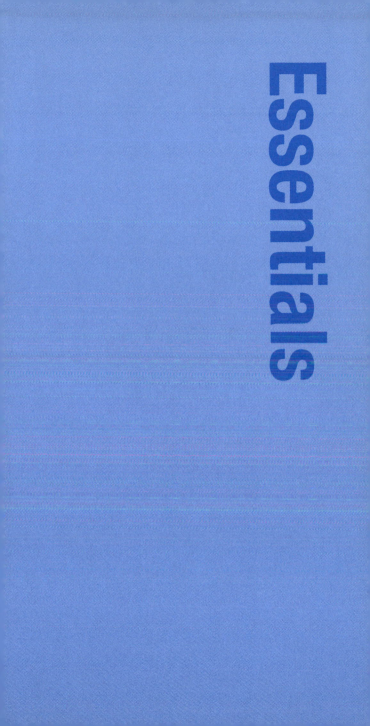

# Essentials

# Arrival

All **flights** arrive into Grantley Adams International Airport, located on the south coast about eight miles east of Bridgetown, and within easy striking distance of all the main south coast resorts. Buses run between the airport and Bridgetown roughly every half-hour (B$1.50), stopping at or near most of the south coast resorts en route. Services to the resorts on the west coast are less frequent. Alternatively, there are numerous car rental outlets at the airport, while taxis cost around B$40 to the hotels in St James on the west coast, B$50 to Speightstown, B$20 to Crane Bay and B$25 to the resorts in the southwest.

The occasional **cruise ship** arrives at the Deep Water Harbour just north of Bridgetown, from where taxis are always available to ferry passengers around the island.

# Information

Both the **Barbados Tourism Authority** office at Harbour Road in Bridgetown (☎427 2623, 🖷426 4080) and their desk at the airport stock plenty of information on the country, including brochures on the main tourist attractions and upcoming events, and a good road map. Most of the car rental outlets will also provide you with a free map of the island upon rental, and there are, of course, the maps at the back of this book.

Barbados has no detailed listings magazine for music, theatre or cinema, though the free fortnightly magazine *Sunseeker* – available from the tourist office and some hotels – carries information on many of the events. Keep an eye also on the daily papers and on flyers posted up around the island; local radio stations (see p.141) also advertise major events.

## Useful websites

🌐 **www.barbados.org** The official site of the Barbados Tourism Authority has information on forthcoming events as well as details and prices of places to stay and eat, companies offering sightseeing tours and car rental outfits, many of which you can book with through the site.

🌐 **www.barbadosturfclub.com** A good site for horseracing enthusiasts, with all the latest news from the Garrison Savannah racetrack, though an excellent links section features plenty of general island sites as well.

🌐 **www.cricket.org** Barbados cries out for its own cricketing website, but for now the best way to find out about forthcoming matches is through this excellent, but generalized, site.

🌐 **www.divebarbados.net** Useful dive site, with descriptions of the main dive opportunities around the island and links

---

### Visas and red tape

All visitors must have a **passport**, valid for at least six months after the date of departure, to enter Barbados. Citizens of Britain, Ireland, the US, Canada, Australia and New Zealand can enter Barbados without a visa and stay for up to three months. In theory, you'll need a return ticket or proof of onward travel and you might also be asked to show that you have sufficient funds to cover your stay. If you want to extend your stay beyond three months, contact the Immigration office in Bridgetown (☎426 9912).

to dive/accommodation deals.

Ⓦ **www.funbarbados.com** Informative island guide, with some excellent deals on accommodation and car rental.

Ⓦ **www.icerecords.com** One of the best of several sites dedicated to the music of leading Bajan and other Caribbean artists. Chock full of artist profiles and industry news.

Ⓦ **www.insandoutsofbarbados.com** Online version of *Barbados Ins and Outs* magazine, which you'll find in many hotel rooms. Focuses largely on places to stay and eat, but has some interesting features on the main tourist attractions.

Ⓦ **www.nationnews.com** The island's daily paper provides the best site for contemporary news, sport and features, as well as the latest weather news.

# Island transport and tours

Inexpensive, speedy buses and minibuses run around the island's coasts and into almost every nook and cranny of the interior. An even better way of seeing Barbados is to rent a car for a couple of days and cruise around at your own pace – though this isn't cheap. If you just want to make the odd excursion or short trip, it can work out cheaper to take a taxi or even to go on a guided tour.

## By bus

Blue government **buses** and smaller, privately owned **minibuses** run all over the island and offer particularly good services up and down the west coast – between Bridgetown and Speightstown – and along the south coast, between Bridgetown and Silver Sands. The destination is written on a board on the front of the bus and fares are a flat rate of B$1.50 – try to have the right change ready. The red and white bus stops are never far apart, and marked "To City" and "Out of City", depending on whether the bus is going towards or away from Bridgetown. If you're not clear where you're headed, other passengers will invariably help you out.

Privately owned white minivans known as **route taxis**, identified by the ZR on their numberplates, also operate like minibuses, packing in passengers and stopping anywhere en route where they see potential custom. They're particularly numerous on the south coast and the fare, as on the buses, is B$1.50. Many Bajans don't use route taxis because they consider the drivers to be reckless and totally uninterested in passenger comfort.

## By car

The roads on Barbados are mostly good and distances are small. Driving is on the left. Rental prices, however, are fairly high, starting at around B$80 per day or B$500 per week, for the mini **mokes** (open-sided buggies) that you'll see all over the island, and a little more for a regular car. Third party **insurance** is included in the price; if you don't have a credit card that offers free collision damage insurance, you'll have to pay another B$15–20 per day if you want to cover potential damage to the rental car.

When renting, you'll have to obtain a local **licence** (B$10), and you'll need a current **licence** from your home country or an international driver's licence and, normally, a **credit card** to make a security deposit. Check the car fully to ensure that every dent, scratch or missing part is inventoried before you set off. When returning the car, don't forget to collect any credit card deposit slips.

The big international operators do not operate out of Barbados and, since car rental companies on the island are all local, it can be easier to organize things once you've arrived. Reliable firms include Coconut (☎437 0297), Jones (☎426 5030), Mangera (☎436 0562) and National (☎422 0603). Each of these should deliver the car to your hotel.

# By taxi

Finding a **taxi** in Barbados – identifiable from a Z on their numberplates – is rarely a problem. They are particularly recommended if you're travelling around at night, when the roads – sometimes poorly lit and busy – can be somewhat daunting. The best option is to ask your hotel or guesthouse to recommend someone local; if they can't help, try one of the following. Bridgetown: Independence ☎426 0090 or Nelson's ☎429 4421; Hastings: Caribbee ☎427 0240; Rockley: Rockley Taxi ☎435 8211; St James: Sunset Crest ☎432 0367.

Fares are regulated but there are no meters, so agree on the fare before you get in the car. Most taxi drivers are scrupulously honest, but you might want to check at your hotel on the appropriate fare for your destination.

# By bike and motorcycle

Since Barbados is so small, and there are few steep inclines, it would seem like ideal cycling territory, yet this mode of transport has never really caught on, and cycle hire options are limited. However, you can normally get a bike from Dread

or Dead in Hastings (☎228 4785) and Flex in Speightstown (☎419 2453 or 231 1518). Hiring a scooter or motorcycle is also possible – prices normally start at around B$80 per day or B$420 per week – and can be a fantastic way of touring around, though you'll need to watch out for drivers on the main roads. Try Caribbean Scooters, Waterfront Marina, Bridgetown (☎436 8522).

# Tours

There are various local companies who offer island-wide sightseeing tours, either to a set itinerary or customized to your needs for those who don't fancy driving. Remember to check whether the price includes entrance fees to the various attractions. Your hotel may also organize tours direct. If you can't get a good price from any of the companies below, you could check with some of the taxi operators (see above).

## Tour companies

**Bajan Helicopters** ☎431 0069. Short but spectacular helicopter tours of the island from the heliport in Bridgetown. A twenty-minute ride costs B$145, thirty minutes costs B$245.
**EL Scenic Tours** ☎424 9108. Offers three well-priced tours daily: Harrison's Cave for B$50; Harrison's Cave and the Flower Forest for B$80; and Harrison's Cave, the Flower Forest, Bathsheba and St John's Parish Church for B$85. All prices include entrance fees.

## Trips to other islands

LIAT (☎434 5428) runs flights to all the nearby islands as well as into Venezuela in South America. Fares start at around B$250 for round-trip flights to St Lucia, St Vincent and Grenada, and most will allow you one or more free stopovers en route. Tickets are sold at a multitude of travel agents island-wide.

If you really want to splash out, note that a couple of companies offer **day-trips** to the beautiful Grenadine islands, with an early morning flight to Union Island followed by a catamaran trip through several more of the cays, plus plenty of snorkelling and a buffet lunch. Prices start at B$490 per person, rising to B$700 if you want to stop off at Mustique for breakfast and a tour of the houses of the rich and famous. Contact Chantours (☎432 5591) or Grenadine Tours (☎435 8451).

**Island Safari** ☎429 5337. One of the more organized tour groups, and probably the most popular, offering excellent, informative Land Rover cruises of the island – heading into the wilder places away from the established "sights" – for between B$80 and B$115, including lunch, depending on how much exploring they're doing on a particular day.

**Johnson's Stables** ☎426 5181. Can provide a car and driver to take you around for half a day for around B$45 per person (entry fees extra); there's normally a minimum of three to four people, though they'll waive this at quiet times. Boyce's Tours (☎425 5366) offer a similar deal, and both companies will be happy to customize an itinerary for you.

# Money

Barbados is not a particularly cheap country to visit, and prices for many items are at least as much as you'd pay at home. Negotiation on price is generally frowned on – taxi rates, for example, are normally fixed – but, particularly during the off-season (April–Nov), it can be worth asking for a reduced rate for items like accommodation or car rental.

## Currency

The island's unit of currency is the **Barbados dollar** (B$), which comes in bills of 2, 5, 10, 20, 50 and 100 dollars, and coins of 1, 5, 10 and 25 cents, and $1. The rate of exchange is fixed at B$2 to US$1 – though you'll get a fraction less when you exchange money – and the US dollar is usually accepted in payment for goods and services.

Prices are normally quoted in B$, with the exception of accommodation, which is almost universally quoted in US$, and we have followed this practice in the Guide.

## Costs

Apart from the flight, accommodation is likely to be the major expense of your trip. The least expensive double rooms start at around US$25 (£13/B$50), though most of the cheaper options cost around US$35–40 (£19–21/B$70–80) in winter, US$30–35 (£16–19/B$60–70) in summer. For something more salubrious, and along the west coast, expect to pay at least US$70–80 (£37–43/B$140–160)

in winter, US$50–60 (£27–32/B$100–120) in summer. Rooms apart, if you travel around on public transport and buy your food from supermarkets and eat at the cheaper cafés, you can just about survive on a **daily budget** of around US$20 (£11/B$40) per day. Upgrading to one decent meal out, the occasional museum or plantation house visit and a bit of evening entertainment, expect to spend a more realistic US$30–40 (£16–21/B$60–80); after that, the sky's the limit.

## Travellers' cheques and credit cards

Easily the safest and most convenient method of carrying money abroad is in the form of **travellers' cheques** and, while sterling and other currencies are accepted in the island's banks, US dollars travellers' cheques are the most convenient ones to have. They are available for a small commission from most banks, and from branches of American Express and Thomas Cook; make sure you keep the purchase agreement and a record of cheque serial numbers safe and separate from the cheques themselves. Once in Barbados, they can be cashed at banks (you'll need your passport or other photo ID to validate them) for a small charge.

Major **credit cards** – American Express, Visa, Mastercard – are widely accepted, but don't necessarily expect the smaller hotels and restaurants to take them. You can also use the cards to get cash advances at most banks, though you'll pay both commission to the bank and hefty interest to your credit card company. Many banks, including Royal Bank of Canada, have ATMs for those with Visa and Plus system cards; these can be used to withdraw local cash.

## Banks and exchange

Banking hours are generally Monday through Thursday 8am–3pm and Fri 8am–5pm; branches of the Caribbean Commercial Bank are also open Saturday 9am–noon. Many hotels will also exchange money, though if you're chaging anything other than US dollars the rate is usually a bit worse than at the banks.

## Emergency cash

If you run out of money, you can arrange a telegraphic transfer to most of the banks in Barbados from your home bank account or that of a friend or family member. Bear in mind that such a transfer will attract hefty commission at both ends, so treat this very much as a last resort.

# Accommodation

There is no shortage of accommodation in Barbados, ranging from some of the world's very best hotels to simple and inexpensive guest houses. Heading up the **west coast** – traditionally the swankier side of the island – you'll find most of the pricier options, many of them concentrated around the lovely Paynes Bay or on either side of Holetown, but thinning out considerably as you continue north towards Speightstown. On the **southwest and southeast coasts**, where the beaches are just as good (or better), accommodation is much more reasonably priced, with plenty of good-value options, particularly around Worthing and St Lawrence Gap, and other places that cater specifically for a younger crowd, like the windsurfing hotels in Maxwell and Silver Sands. There are very few options elsewhere on the island. A handful of small, mostly long-established hotels still do a light trade on the wild **east coast**, around Bathsheba and Cattlewash, but there is as yet nowhere to stay in the centre or north of the island.

## All-inclusives

The latest trend in hotel accommodation in the Caribbean has been towards "all-inclusive" hotels, and Barbados is no exception. The simple concept behind these places is that you pay a single price that covers your room, all meals and, normally, all drinks and watersports, so you can "leave your wallet at home".

---

### Accommodation prices

The accommodation prices in the Guide refer to the cost per night of the cheapest double rooms in each establishment during the winter, or high, season (mid-Dec to mid-April). Room prices on the island are usually quoted in US dollars, and we have followed this practice in the Guide.

Nearly every hotel has a significant difference between its winter and summer prices, and for many places we have given both categories, with the winter price first. Bear in mind that if you book for a week or more, particularly as part of a package, prices will normally be much lower.

If you are thinking of booking an all-inclusive, focus on what you specifically want out of it. *Almond Beach* and *Club Rockley*, for example, have several restaurants and bars, so you don't have to face the same menu every night; smaller places like *Escape* offer less variety, but a bit more space on the beach. Remember, too, that the allure of drinking seven types of "free" cocktail in a night or stuffing your face at the "free" buffet quickly fades, and if you want to get out and sample Barbados' myriad great restaurants and bars, you're better off steering clear of all-inclusives.

## Private homes, apartments and villas

A number of families offer bed and breakfast in their homes starting at around $20 per person; branches of the Barbados Tourism Authority (see p.127) normally have lists, or you can contact Bajan Holidays Inc. in Bridgetown (℡ and ℻ 438 4043). The latter also has details of apartments and villas available for rent, as do Alleyne, Aguilar & Altman (℡432 0840, 🌐www.aaaltman.com) and Ronald Stoute & Sons (℡423 6800, 🌐www.ronstoute.com). Prices start at around US$500/800 for a one-bedroom/two-bedroom villa for a week in the summer, roughly double in winter. There are, however, no youth hostels on the island and camping is banned.

# Communications

Calling within Barbados is simple – most hotels provide a **telephone** in each room and local calls are usually free (though check first). You'll also see Bartel phone booths all over the island, and these can be used for local and international calls. Most of the booths take phonecards only – these are available at hotels, post offices and some shops and supermarkets. For finding numbers, hotel rooms and phone booths often have a directory; failing that, call directory assistance on ℡119. To make a **collect call**, dial ℡01, plus the area code (minus the initial zero) and number you wish to reach.

## Mail

Barbados's **postal service** is extremely efficient. The General Post Office in Bridgetown (Mon–Fri 7.30am–5pm) has *poste restante* facilities for receiving mail. There are also branches across the island, in the larger towns and villages and at the airport (Mon–Fri 8am–3.15pm), and you can buy stamps

---

### Dialling codes

#### To call Barbados from abroad

Dial your international access code (see below)
+ 246 + seven digit number
UK ℡001
USA ℡011
Canada ℡011
Australia ℡0011
New Zealand ℡00

#### To call abroad from Barbados

Dial the country code (see below)
+ number (omitting the initial zero if there is one)
UK ℡011 44
USA ℡01
Canada ℡01
Australia ℡011 61
New Zealand℡011 64

and send mail at many of the hotels. Postal rates are reasonable: to the US and Canada, air mail is B$0.90, postcards B$0.60; to the UK, air mail is B$1.10, postcards $0.70.

## Email

If you want to check **email** or just surf the Internet, many hotels will let you use their computers for free or for a nominal charge. Alternatively, there are a fair number of Internet cafés dotted around the island: in St Lawrence Gap, Bean & Bagel (see p.75) offers Internet access from B$6 for 15 minutes; in Holetown, Global Business Centre (a stall in the West Coast Mall) charges B$5 for 10 minutes' access.

# Food and drink

As you'd expect, fresh seafood is the island's speciality: snapper, barracuda and dolphin fish (not the porpoise), as well as fresh prawns and lobster. Most popular of all, though, is the **flying fish** – virtually a Bajan national emblem. The fish doesn't really fly; accelerating up to 65kph it shoots out of the water and, extending its lateral fins like wings, glides through the air for up to thirty metres, usually to escape underwater pursuit.

Look out, too, for traditional Bajan dishes: the national dish is **cou-cou** (a cornmeal and okra pudding) and saltfish, and you'll occasionally find the fabulous **pudding and souse** – steamed sweet potato served with cuts of pork pickled in onion, lime and hot peppers. **Cohobblopot** (also known as pepperpot) is a spicy meat and okra stew. Dishes from the wider Caribbean, such as the fiery Jamaican-style jerk pork or chicken, are also popular.

Vegetarians will have to work a bit to avoid meat or fish. Despite the fantastic selection of vegetables, including the starchy **breadfruit** (best roasted) and the squash-like **christophene**, restaurants often don't have even a single vegetarian option, in which case you'll have to negotiate. Watch out too for the ubiquitous **peas and rice** (rice cooked with a variety of peas or beans) that accompanies many main dishes, as a piece of salted pork is usually chucked into the pot for added flavour.

For snacks, you'll find **cutters** (bread rolls with a meat or cheese filling) and coconut bread in many bars and rum shops, and more substantial **rotis** (flat, unleavened bread wrapped around a filling of curried meat or vegetables) are also widely available. Less frequently seen outside a Bajan home, but worth keeping an eye open for, are **conkies**, made from pumpkin, sweet potato, cornmeal and coconut, mixed and steamed in banana leaves.

Finally, don't miss out on the superb local **fruits**, from mangoes and paw paws to the more exotic sapodillas and sweetsops.

## Drink

**Rum** (see p.64) is the liquor of choice for many Bajans. The local **beer** is Banks, a light golden lager made from a blend of barley and hops, by far the most popular brew island-wide. **Wine** is an expensive option, though you'll occasionally find Californian whites and reds at reasonable prices.

Hundreds of tiny **rum bars** dot the island; they are an integral part of Bajan social life, and are great places to stop off for a drink and a chat. On the coast, you'll find fewer places that cater specifically to drinkers but, all-inclusives apart, most hotels and restaurants will welcome you for a drink even if you're not staying or eating there. Holetown and St Lawrence Gap are particularly good for bar-hopping.

# Festivals, events and public holidays

The main festival in Barbados is the summertime Crop Over, which reaches its climax on Kadooment Day when the festival monarchs are crowned. There are plenty of other events to distract you from the beach as well, for which the local tourist board (see p.127) has full details – alternatively, call the appropriate number below.

## Festival calendar

### January

**Barbados Jazz Festival** ☎429 2084.
**Barbados Windsurfing Championships** ☎426 5837.
**Busta Cup Cricket Competition** ☎426 5128.

### February

**Holetown Festival** ☎430 7300 (see below).

### March

**Holders opera season** (see p.85).
**Oistins Fish Festival** ☎428 6738.
**Test cricket** ☎426 5128 (see p.140).

### April

**Congaline Carnival** ☎424 0909 (see below).

### May

**Gospelfest** ☎430 7300 (see below).

### July–August

**Crop Over Festival** (see below).

### October

**Barbados International Triathlon** ☎435 7000.

### November

**Caribbean Surfing Championship** ☎435 6377.
**Festival of Creative Arts** ☎424 0909.

### December

**Barbados Road Race Series**

## Crop Over

This festival, held every summer, traditionally celebrated the completion of the sugar harvest and the end of months of exhausting work for the field-labourers on the sugar estates. As with many countries' carnival, which immediately precedes a period of fasting, Crop Over carried a frenzied sense of "enjoy-yourself-while-you-may", as workers knew that earnings would now be minimal until the next crop. Alongside the flags, dances and rum-drinking, the symbol of the festival was "Mr Harding" – a scarecrow-like figure stuffed with the dried leaves of the sugar cane – who was paraded around and introduced to the manager of the sugar plantation.

Though Crop Over has lost some of its significance since the 1960s, with sugar replaced by tourism as the country's main industry, it's still the island's main festival and an excuse for an extended party. Things start slowly in early July, with craft exhibitions and band rehearsals, heating up in late July and early August with street parades, concerts and competitions between the tuk bands, steel bands and – most importantly – the battle for the title of calypso monarch, dominated in recent decades by the Mighty Gabby and Red Plastic Bag who, between them, have won nine times in the last thirty years.

## Congaline Carnival

Held during the last week in April, Congaline Carnival puts on a varied program of mostly local music that includes soca, reggae, steelpan and calypso. Daily shows are held from mid-afternoon to

## Public holidays

| | |
|---|---|
| New Year's Day | Jan 1 |
| Errol Barrow Day | Jan 21 |
| Good Friday | Friday before Easter Sunday |
| Easter Monday | day after Easter Sunday |
| National Heroes Day | April 28 |
| Labour Day | May 1 |
| Whit Monday | eighth Mon after Easter |
| Emancipation Day | Aug 1 |
| Kadooment Day | first Mon in Aug |
| United Nations Day | first Mon in Oct |
| Independence Day | Nov 30 |
| Christmas Day | Dec 25 |
| Boxing Day | Dec 26 |

late evening, usually at Dover pasture near St Lawrence Gap, and other events around the island conclude with a May Day parade through Bridgetown from the Garrison Savannah to the Spring Garden Highway.

## Holetown Festival

Commemorating the first settlement of Barbados at Holetown in February 1627, the week-long festival begins in mid-February, with the opening celebrations taking place at the Holetown Monument. The festival showcases local arts and crafts as well as Barbadian culture and history, and events typically include fashion shows, street parades, concerts and sporting events.

## Gospelfest

This lively festival reflects the important role that gospel music plays in the spiritual lives of many Barbadians. Bringing together some of the top gospel singers and bands from North America, the Caribbean and Barbados, the festival also includes reggae, calypso, jazz and soul.

# Shopping

If you want to take home something authentically Bajan, check out the craft stalls at **Pelican Village** (see p.58) in Bridgetown. Alternatively, wait for the vendors to find you – they hang out on the most popular beaches, particularly Accra Beach on the south coast, and regularly set up stands selling clothing, carved wooden figurines and Haitian-style paintings of markets and other traditional scenes. The **Best of Barbados** gift shops dotted around the island also sell decent-quality souvenirs, from books and prints to T-shirts and rum – the latter being perhaps the most authentically Bajan souvenir of all (see p.64).

Other than that, you're largely restricted to the familiar **duty-free shops**, with a massive array in Broad Street in Bridgetown (open Mon–Fri 8.30am–4.30pm, Sat 8.30am–1pm). Be sure to take your passport or air ticket as proof of visitor status.

# Ocean and beach safety

You'll find that the only real threat to your physical welfare is the intense **Caribbean sun**. Many visitors get badly sunburned on the first day and suffer for the rest of the trip. To avoid their fate, it's advisable to wear a strong sunscreen at all times. Unreconstructed sun-worshippers should at least avoid the heat of the day between 11.30am and 2.30pm.

While you're on the beach, steer clear of the **manchineel trees**, recognizable by their shiny green leaves and the small, crab apple–like fruits that will be scattered around. The fruit is poisonous and, when it rains, the bark releases a sap that will cause blisters if it drips on you.

The sea, too, poses a handful of threats. Don't worry about the rarely seen sharks or barracudas, but watch out for the occasional spiny, black **sea urchins**, which are easily missed if you're walking over a patch of sea grass. If you step on one and can't get the spines out, you'll need medical help.

# Sport and leisure

The water-sports fan is well catered for in Barbados, with plenty of operators offering excellent diving, snorkelling, waterskiing and similar activities. Windsurfing and surfing are also world-class, particularly on the southeast and east coasts respectively.

There are plenty of land-based sports facilities, too, including good golf courses, horse-riding stables, and the opportunity for some excellent hiking. Finally, for spectators, there is international cricket at the Kensington Oval (see p.59) between January and April each year, and horseracing at the Garrison Savannah (see p.61).

## Scuba-diving and snorkelling

**Scuba-diving** is excellent on the coral reefs around Barbados, with the good sites all off the calm west and southwest coasts, from Maycocks Bay in the north right round to Castle Bank near St Lawrence Gap. The island has plenty of reputable dive operators, most of whom will lay on transport to and from your hotel. Prices can vary dramatically between diveshops – always call around for the best deal – but reckon on around B\$100 for a single tank dive, B\$150 for a two-tank dive and B\$120 for a night dive, including use of equipment.

Beginners can get a feel for diving by taking a half-day **resort course**, involving basic theory, a shallow water (or pool) demonstration and a single dive. The course costs around B\$150, and allows you to continue to dive with the people who taught you, though not with any other operator.

Full **open-water certification** – involving theory, tests, training dives and four full dives – takes three to four days and is rather more variable in price – expect to pay B\$700–800, depending on the time of year and how busy the operator is. Serious divers should consider a package deal; these may simply cover three or five two-tank dives (roughly B\$400 and B\$700 respectively), or may also include accommodation and diving. Prices for these can be pretty good value, with savings of up to twenty percent, particularly outside the winter season.

**Snorkelling** is excellent, too, especially off the west coast, where there are plenty of good coralheads just offshore and sea turtles in the turtle grass near the *Lone Star Motel* and *Cobblers Cove Hotel* (see pp.95 & 96). If you want to go out to sea, find one of the several dive operators who take snorkellers on their dive trips – reckon on spending B\$20–30 for an outing, including equipment. Many top hotels provide guests with free snorkelling gear, but if you're not at one of these, finding the equipment can be expensive – try the outfits listed within each Places chapter – and you may want to bring a mask and snorkel with you.

## Scuba-diving companies

**Dive Barbados** Next to Lone Star restaurant ☎ 422 3133,
ⓦ www.divebarbados.net.
**The Dive Shop** Aquatic Gap ☎ 426 9947,
ⓦ www.divebds.com.
**Hightide Watersports**
Sandy Lane hotel ☎ 432 0931,
ⓦ www.divehightide.com.
**One on one scuba** Sandy Beach Island Resort, Worthing ☎ 435 9811,
ⓦ www.one-on-one-scuba.com.

# Boats trips

There is no shortage of boat trips to be made around Barbados, with the emphasis – not, it must be said, everyone's cup of tea – normally on being part of a big crowd all having a fun time together. Most of the **cruise boats** charge a single price, which will depend on whether the trip includes a meal and/or "free" drinks. As the alcohol kicks in, people get into dancing mode with the live or canned music and, depending on the boat, you can walk the plank or swing from ropes into the sea. The **catamarans** offer similar trips, though usually with a smaller number of people on board and less in the way of entertainment. All these boats sail out of Bridgetown's Shallow Harbour, but most will pick up guests from any of the major resorts.

## Boat companies

**Cool Runnings** Boats depart from Shallow Harbour ☎ 436 0911.
This 45-foot catamaran offers five-hour lunchtime snorkelling cruises, taking in the turtles near the *Lone Star Motel* and a shallow wreck just offshore, and four-hour sunset and snorkelling cruises along the coast. A maximum of 26 people are allowed onboard, and food and drink are included in the price of B$130.
**Harbour Master** Boats depart from Shallow Harbour ☎ 427 7245.
Massive four-decker boat that runs regular day tours, taking you up the coast to a beach for chilling out or snorkelling, with a buffet lunch and free drinks (Tues & Thurs 11am–4pm; B$140). It also runs evening trips (Tues & Thurs 6–10pm), with a floor show, a live band, dinner and drinks all included in the price, and a cheaper option (Sun 5–9pm; B$35), where you pay for your food and drinks and a DJ provides the entertainment.
**Jolly Roger** Boats depart from Shallow Harbour ☎ 430 0900,
ⓦ www.tallshipscruises.com. Tues, Thurs & Sat 10am–2pm. B$123.
Sleek, two-sailed "pirate ship" running west coast lunch cruises, with the emphasis on drinking and dancing up on the top deck, walking the plank and swinging from the yard-arm into the sea.
**Limbo Lady** Boats depart from Shallow Harbour ☎ 420 5418.
A classic 44-foot yacht that operates lunchtime and sunset cruises (B$102–134), with snorkelling on the lunchtime cruise and champagne on the Tuesday evening sunset cruise.

## Atlantis Submarine

A rare opportunity to ride in a submarine and get a taste of underwater adventure without getting wet. A boat takes you out of the Bridgetown harbour to board the sub, which then submerges 30–45m, cruising slowly above the sea-bed for around thirty minutes before it rises to rejoin the "mother ship". Everyone has a seat by a porthole, and spectacular views of the fish and the coral, backed by a commentary on what you're seeing from the co-pilot. Boats depart from Shallow Harbour. Tickets are B$165 per person. Call ☎ 436 8929 for details.

**Tiami** Boats depart from Shallow Harbour ☎ 430 0900, 🌐 www.tallshipscruises .com.

Tiami has three catamarans that take west coast lunch cruises, where the four-hour trip includes several beach/snorkelling stops as well as your food and drink for B$140. A sunset cruise is also available for around $90.

# Windsurfing and surfing

Barbados hosts regular **windsurfing** tournaments around Silver Sands on the southeast coast, which is reckoned to be as good for windsurfers and kitesurfers as anywhere in the Caribbean. Several of the hotels in the area cater mainly or exclusively for windsurfers; boards can be rented beside the *Silver Rock Hotel* (☎ 428 2866) or at the *Silver Sands Hotel* (☎ 428 6001), and cost around B$40 per hour, B$70 for half a day, or from the windsurfing schools like Club Mistral (☎ 428 6001, 🌐 www.clubmistral barbados.com), whose prices for coaching border on the extortionate. Elsewhere on the island, there are no rental outlets but many of the hotels have their own windsurfers, which you can use – if you're staying there – for no extra cost.

**Surfing** is also excellent, particularly on the east coast at the Bathsheba "soup-bowl" (see p.121). Boards can be rented from the *Round House Inn* in Bathsheba, and you can buy them at some branches of the Cave Shepherd department store (☎ 431 2121). Useful information can be gleaned from the Barbados Surfing Association (☎ 228 5117, 🌐 www .bsasurf.org) and from the website of the Bajan Surf Bungalow in Bathsheba (🌐 www.bajansurfbungalow.com).

# Fishing

Fishing is a way of life in Barbados, both as an industry and as a sport, and if you are at all interested, the island is an incomparable place to try your hand. Various charter boats offer deep-sea

fishing trips on which you can go after wahoo, tuna, barracuda and, if you're lucky, marlin and other sailfish. Prices for a group of up to six people start at around B$500 for a half-day, B$1000 for a whole day, including rods, bait, food, drink and transport from your hotel. If you are not part of a group, operators will fit you in with another party if they can, and charge around B$180 for a half-day. Regular **operators** include Billfisher II (☎ 431 0741), Honey Bea III (☎ 428 5344) and Blue Marlin Charters (☎ 436 4322), but if you hunt around at dock-side, particularly in Bridgetown, you can find plenty of others. Information on fishing tournaments held on the island is available from the Barbados Game Fishing Association (🌐 www.barbados gamefishing.com).

# Other water sports

If you're after **waterskiing**, **jet-ski** rides or a speedy tow on an inflatable banana, most hotels can find a reputable operator for you – expect to pay around B$45 for fifteen minutes of waterskiing and half that for banana rides or jet-ski rental. Hightide Watersports (☎ 432 0931), in Sandy Lane Bay, is one of the most trustworthy operators. Another is Charles Watersports (☎ 428 9550) on Dover Beach. You'll also find guys with speedboats on many of the west coast beaches, though less so on the south coast where the water is often a bit too choppy. Bear in mind that though these operators are often cheaper, many of them are unlicensed and uninsured, and don't go with anyone unless you feel comfortable with their operation.

Similarly, you'll find locals offering trips on a **hobie-cat** (a mini-catamaran) on many of the beaches; they'll usually want to crew the boat themselves unless you can convince them you're an expert. There's a good range of kit, including pedal boats and kayaks, at *The Boatyard* on Bay Street in Bridgetown (☎ 436 2622).

Finally, Falcon (☎ 419 0579, 🌐 www.parasailingwiththefalcon.com.bb) offers ten-minute **parasailing** trips – you're towed behind a boat on a parachute, then winched back aboard – for B$90 per person, and they will pick you up from any west coast beach.

# Hiking and biking

Some of the best and most scenic **hiking** on Barbados is along the beaches, particularly the east coast stretches between Martin's Bay and Bath and between Bathsheba and Cattlewash (see p.121). Organized hikes are arranged by the Barbados National Trust (☎426 2421) whose guides every Sunday take hikers around areas like the Garrison Savannah (p.61), the Graeme Hall Swamp (p.68) and along the excellent Arbib Nature and Heritage Trail around old Speightstown. If you want to hike inland, get hold of the 1:50,000 topographic map, available from the Lands and Survey Department, Jemmott Street, Bridgetown (☎426 3959).

**Bike tours** are another good way of seeing the island. The Highland Adventure Centre organises very enjoyable one-and-a-half-hour trips (☎438 8069) around Mount Hillaby and down to the Atlantic Coast, while Bonnie Cole-Wilson at the *Casuarina Beach Club* (p.72) leads early-morning bike trips for guests at her hotel and sometimes allows others to come along.

# Golf

There are two eighteen-hole golf courses open to the public in Barbados: one at Durants on the southwest coast and one on the west coast at Sandy Lane. Particularly in high season, it can be difficult to get a tee time at either course and it's worth planning ahead. The other major course, Royal Westmoreland, is only open to members and guests staying at certain of the more exclusive hotels. There is also a decent nine-hole course at Rockley on the southwest coast.

### Golf courses

**Barbados Academy of Golf** Balls ☎420 7405. If you fancy some practice or small-scale fun, the Barbados Academy

of Golf has a public driving range and an eighteen-hole miniature golf course.

**Barbados Golf Club** Durants ☎428 8463, ✆www.barbadosgolfclub.com. Green fees are B$150–200, club rental a further B$50–60.

**Club Rockley Barbados** Rockley ☎435 7873, ✆www.clubrockley.com. Green fees are B$60–110, club rental an additional B$20.

**Sandy Lane** Sandy Lane Bay ☎432 1311, ✆432 2954, ✆www.sandylane.com. Beautifully landscaped 6000m course. Green fees are B$150–200, club rental a further B$50–60.

# Equestrian sports

Barbados has a lively equestrian tradition. There are regular Saturday races at the Garrison Savannah racetrack (see p.61), and at Sandy Lane in March. The country has several polo fields as well; the most prestigious of them, at Holders House (see p.85), holds matches twice a week from September to March.

Not surprisingly, the island has stables offering **riding tours** that start at around B$75. Good trips are organized by the Caribbean International Riding Centre (☎422 7433 or 420 1246), which offers three options: an hour's tour of the Scotland district, a ninety-minute ride down to the beach, and a two-and-a-half-hour trip to the beach and back. Also worthwhile is the riding tour led by the Highland Adventure Centre (☎438 8069), located in the St Thomas parish. The hour-and-a-quarter ride (B$120) travels past small villages and through sugar cane fields, in which green monkeys can often be spotted searching for food.

# Clay pigeon and pistol shooting

Set in 70 acres just inland from the south coast, **Kendal Sporting** is a small members club that welcomes visitors for clay pigeon and pistol shooting from Tuesday to Sunday, 10.30am–5pm. Coaching and safety advice are available to all, and the levels can be set from beginner to expert. Expect to pay from B\$50 upwards for a gun and ammunition. There's a good restaurant and welcoming pool as well, and non-shooters are welcome.

# Cricket

If you're in Barbados for any length of time, you'll find it almost impossible to avoid the subject of cricket; more, per-haps, than anywhere else on earth, the game is *the* national passion. It was intro-duced to the island by the British military in the second half of the nineteenth cen-tury and today, alongside Jamaica and Trinidad, the island is one of the Big Three Caribbean cricketing nations. If you get the chance, catch a day of international cricket at the main ground in Bridgetown (known as the Kensington Oval; see p.59). While the rest of the island slows to a near standstill, the otherwise stately stadium is transformed into a fairground, with music blaring, vendors hawking jerk chicken and Banks beer and a noisy crowd debating the finer points of the game. Listen out for the local cricketing lingo – a fielder placed out near the boundary, for example, is "in the country" – and for the lasting hoots of derision if anyone should spill a catch.

## The rules of cricket

Though the laws of cricket are complex the basics are by no means as Byzantine as the game's detractors make out. The following are the bare rudiments of a game whose beauty lies in the subtlety of its skills and tactics.

There are **two teams** of eleven play-ers. A team wins by scoring more runs than the other team and dismissing all the opposition – in other words, a team could score many runs more than the opposition, but still not win if the last enemy batsman doggedly stays "**in**" (hence ensuring a draw). The match is divided into **innings**, when one team bats and the other fields. The number of innings varies depending on the type of competition: one-day matches have one per team, Test matches have two.

The aim of the fielding side is to limit the runs scored and get the batsmen "**out**". Two players from the batting side are on the pitch at any one time. The bowling side has a bowler, a wicketkeep-er and nine fielders. Each inning is divid-ed into overs, consisting of six deliveries, after which the wicketkeeper changes ends, the bowler is changed and the fielders move positions.

The batsmen **score runs** either by run-ning up and down from wicket to wicket (one length = one run), or by hitting the ball over the boundary rope, scoring four runs if it crosses the boundary having touched the ground, and six runs if it flies over. The main ways a batsman can be dismissed are: by being "**clean bowled**", where the bowler dislodges the bails of the wicket (the horizontal pieces of wood resting on top of the stumps); by being "**run out**", which is when one of the field-ing side dislodges the bails with the ball while the batsman is running between the wickets; by being caught, which is when any of the fielding side catches the ball after the batsman has hit it and before it touches the ground; or "**lbw**" (leg before wicket), where the batsman blocks with his leg a delivery that would otherwise have hit his stumps.

# Directory

**Airport departure tax** Departure tax is presently B$25, payable at the airport when you leave, in local currency only.

**Banks** Bridgetown: Barclays, Broad Street and Lower Broad Street; Scotiabank, Broad Street; Barbados National Bank, Broad Street and Fairchild Street. Hastings: Caribbean Commercial Bank in Hastings Place. Worthing: Scotiabank beside the *Sandy Beach Hotel*; CIBC, across the road from Scotiabank in Worthing Plaza. St Lawrence Gap: Royal Bank of Canada by the *Ship Inn* at the west end of the coast road, and Barclays at the other end, near *Shakey's*. Holetown and Speightstown have numerous banks.

**Electric current** The island standard is 110 volts with two-pin sockets, though a few of the older hotels still use 220 volts. Take adaptors for essential items; some upmarket hotels and guest houses have them, but you shouldn't count on it.

**Emergencies** Police ☎211; ambulance ☎511; fire brigade ☎311.

**Hospitals** Bridgetown has the six-hundred-bed public Queen Elizabeth Hospital (☎429 5112) and the private Bayview Hospital (☎436 5446), while smaller health centres and clinics are distributed around the island.

**Laundry** Bridgetown: Lowe's, Roebuck Street ☎426 1235; Steve's, Bay Street ☎427 9119. Hastings: Hastings Village Laundromat, Balmoral Gap ☎429 7079 (Mon, Thurs & Fri 8am–6pm). Worthing: Southshore laundromat ☎435 7438, just across the road from the *Summer Home on Sea* guest house. Holetown: Tropical Laundries, Sunset Crest ☎432 0607. Speightstown: Wish & Wash, Jordan's Complex ☎422 5647 (Mon–Sat 8.30am–5pm).

**Newspapers** The two daily papers, the *Advocate* and the *Nation*, concentrate on domestic news, though there is a token gesture towards international news coverage and, invariably, a big sports section. The *Nation* produces a weekly tourist paper, the *Visitor*, which is worth picking up for its listings.

**Pharmacies** Bridgetown: Cheapside Pharmacy, Cheapside ☎437 2004 (Mon–Fri 7.30am–5.30pm, Sat 7.30am–1.30pm); Knight's, Lower Broad Street ☎426 5196 (daily 8am–1pm). Holetown: Knight's, Sunset Crest (daily 8am–noon). Oistins: Knight's, Southern Plaza (Mon–Sat 8am–8pm, Sun 8am–1pm). Rockley: Lewis' Drug Mart, opposite the *Accra Beach Hotel* (Mon–Fri 9am–6pm, Sat 9am–1pm, Sun 9am–noon). Speightstown: Knight's (Mon–Sat 8am–8pm, Sun 8am–1pm).

**Radio** Radio stations include the public service channel Voice of Barbados (92.9 FM), and the BBS (90.7 FM), both of which carry news, sport, chat shows and music, mostly international hits with a sprinkling of Bajan tunes. The most entertaining show is Voice of Barbados's lively and outspoken phone-in *Down to Brass Tacks*, which goes out every day at 11.30am.

**Time** Barbados is on Eastern Standard Time and four hours behind Greenwich Mean Time.

**Tipping and taxes** Many hotels and restaurants automatically add a service charge of 10 percent, so check your bill to ensure you're not paying twice. At restaurants that don't do this, it's not usually expected but (of course) always appreciated. All prices, whether in restaurants or shops, include 15 percent government tax.

**TV** The local station is shown on channel 8, while many hotels and sports bars carry satellite TV (mostly programmes from North America).

# ROUGH GUIDES
# REFERENCE SERIES

**"The Rough Guides are near-perfect reference works"**
*Philidelphia Enquirer*

History · Internet · Music
Restaurants · Football · Formula 1
Weather · Astronomy · Health
Movies · Videogaming · TV

*DON'T JUST TRAVEL!*

# ROUGH GUIDES TRAVEL...

# ...MUSIC & REFERENCE

West Africa

Zanzibar

Zimbabwe

## Travel Theme guides

First-Time Around the World

First-Time Asia

First-Time Europe

First-Time Latin America

Gay & Lesbian Australia

Skiing & Snowboarding in North America

Travel Online

Travel Health

Walks in London & SE England

Women Travel

## Restaurant guides

French Hotels & Restaurants

London

New York

San Francisco

## Maps

Algarve

Amsterdam

Andalucia & Costa del Sol

Argentina

Athens

Australia

Baja California

Barcelona

Boston

Brittany

Brussels

Chicago

Crete

Croatia

Cuba

Cyprus

Czech Republic

Dominican Republic

Dublin

Egypt

Florence & Siena

Frankfurt

Greece

Guatemala & Belize

Iceland

Ireland

Lisbon

London

Los Angeles

Mexico

Miami & Key West

Morocco

New York City

New Zealand

Northern Spain

Paris

Portugal

Prague

Rome

San Francisco

Sicily

South Africa

Sri Lanka

Tenerife

Thailand

Toronto

Trinidad & Tobago

Tuscany

Venice

Washington DC

Yucatán Peninsula

## Dictionary Phrasebooks

Czech

Dutch

Egyptian Arabic

European

French

German

Greek

Hindi & Urdu

Hungarian

Indonesian

Italian

Japanese

Mandarin Chinese

Mexican Spanish

Polish

Portuguese

Russian

Spanish

Swahili

Thai

Turkish

Vietnamese

## Music Guides

The Beatles

Bob Dylan

Cult Pop

Classical Music

Country Music

Cuban Music

Drum'n'bass

Elvis

Hip Hop

House

Irish Music

Jazz

Music USA

Opera

Reggae

Rock

Techno

World Music (2 vols)

## 100 Essential CDs series

Country

Latin

Opera

Rock

Soul

World Music

## History Guides

China

Egypt

England

France

Greece

India

Ireland

Islam

Italy

Spain

USA

## Reference Guides

Books for Teenagers

Children's Books 0–5

Children's Books 5–11

Cult Fiction

Cult Football

Cult Movies

Cult TV

Digital Stuff

Ethical Shopping

Formula 1

iPods & iTunes

The Internet

Internet Radio

James Bond

Kids' Movies

Lord of the Rings

Man Utd

Muhammad Ali

PCs & Windows

Pregnancy & Birth

Shakespeare

Superheroes

Travel Health

Travel Online

Unexplained Phenomena

The Universe

Videogaming

Weather

Website Directory

ROUGH GUIDES

Also! More than 120 Rough Guide music CDs are available from all good book and record stores. Listen in at www.worldmusic.net

# ROUGH GUIDES
# TRAVEL SERIES

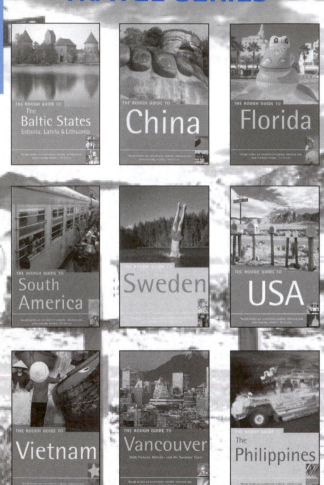

THE ROUGH GUIDE TO
## The Baltic States
Estonia, Latvia & Lithuania

THE ROUGH GUIDE TO
## China

THE ROUGH GUIDE TO
## Florida

THE ROUGH GUIDE TO
## South America

## Sweden

THE ROUGH GUIDE TO
## USA

THE ROUGH GUIDE TO
## Vietnam

THE ROUGH GUIDE TO
## Vancouver
With Victoria, Whistler and the Sunshine Coast

THE ROUGH GUIDE TO
## The Philippines

## Travel guides to more than
## 250 destinations
## from Alaska to Zimbabwe

*smooth travel*

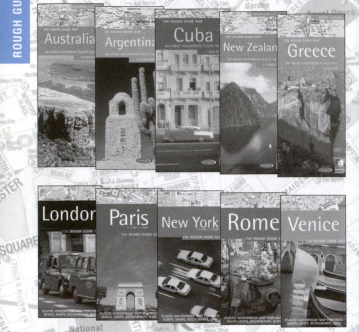

# ROUGH GUIDES
# MUSIC SERIES

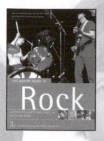

Rock

Opera

Jazz

Hip-Hop

Available November 2004

Reggae

Available August 2004

World Music

Africa, Europe and the Middle East

THE BEATLES

Elvis

Cuban Music

"Rough Guides cover every genre of music.
The books are attractively produced, competitively
priced, meticulously researched and
interestingly written"
The Bookseller, London

Available from your local bookstore
or online at www.roughguides.com

Index and small print

# A Rough Guide to Rough Guides

Barbados DIRECTIONS is published by Rough Guides. The first *Rough Guide to Greece*, published in 1982, was a student scheme that became a publishing phenomenon. The immediate success of the book – with numerous reprints and a Thomas Cook prize shortlisting – spawned a series that rapidly covered dozens of destinations. Rough Guides had a ready market among low-budget backpackers, but soon also acquired a much broader and older readership that relished Rough Guides' wit and inquisitiveness as much as their enthusiastic, critical approach. Everyone wants value for money, but not at any price. Rough Guides soon began supplementing the "rougher" information about hostels and low-budget listings with the kind of detail on restaurants and quality hotels that independent-minded visitors on any budget might expect, whether on business in New York or trekking in Thailand. These days the guides offer recommendations from shoestring to luxury and a large number of destinations around the globe, including almost every country in the Americas and Europe, more than half of Africa and most of Asia and Australasia. Rough Guides now publish:

- Travel guides to more than 200 worldwide destinations
- Dictionary phrasebooks to 22 major languages
- Maps printed on rip-proof and waterproof Polyart™ paper
- Music guides running the gamut from Opera to Elvis
- Reference books on topics as diverse as the Weather and Shakespeare
- World Music CDs in association with World Music Network

Visit **www.roughguides.com** to see our latest publications.

## Publishing information

This 1st edition published August 2004 by **Rough Guides Ltd**, 80 Strand, London WC2R 0RL.
345 Hudson St, 4th Floor, New York, NY 10014, USA.

**Distributed by the Penguin Group**
Penguin Books Ltd, 80 Strand, London WC2R 0RL
Penguin Group (USA), 375 Hudson Street, NY 10014, USA
Penguin Group (Australia), 487 Maroondah Highway, PO Box 257, Ringwood, Victoria 3134, Australia
Penguin Group (Canada), 10 Alcorn Avenue, Toronto, Ontario, Canada M4V 1E4
Penguin Group (NZ), 182–190 Wairau Road, Auckland 10, New Zealand
Typeset in Bembo and Helvetica to an original design by Henry Iles.
Printed and bound in Italy by Graphicom

160pp includes index
A catalogue record for this book is available from the British Library

ISBN 1-84353-320-0

## Help us update

We've gone to a lot of effort to ensure that the first edition of **Barbados DIRECTIONS** is accurate and up-to-date. However, things change – places get "discovered", opening hours are notoriously fickle, restaurants and rooms raise prices or lower standards. If you feel we've got it wrong or left something out, we'd like to know, and if you can remember the address, the price, the time, the phone number, so much the better.

We'll credit all contributions, and send a copy of the next edition (or any other DIRECTIONS guide or Rough Guide if you prefer) for the best letters. Everyone who writes to us and isn't already a subscriber will receive a copy of our full-colour thrice-yearly newsletter. Please mark letters: **"Barbados DIRECTIONS Update"** and send to: Rough Guides, 80 Strand, London WC2R 0RL, or Rough Guides, 4th Floor, 345 Hudson St, New York, NY 10014. Or send an email to **mail@roughguides.com**

Have your questions answered and tell others about your trip at **www.roughguides.atinfopop.com**

## Rough Guide Credits

**Text editor**: Yuki Takagaki
**Layout**: Diana Jarvis
**Photography**: Ian Cumming
**Cartography**: Rajesh Mishra, Ashutosh Bharti and Jai Prakesh Mishra

**Picture research**: Joe Mee
**Proofreader**: Susannah Wight
**Production**: John McKay
**Design**: Henry Iles
**Cover art direction**: Louise Boulton

## The author

**Adam Vaitilingam** is the author of many books on the Caribbean. He lives in Devon.

## Acknowledgements

The author would like to thank Yuki for peerless editing.

## Photo credits

All images © Rough Guides except the following:

Front cover: Bottom Bay © Alamy
Back cover: West Coast © Alamy

p.1    Boats moored at Bridgetown © Bruce Adams/CORBIS
p.2    Sam Lord's Castle Resort Beach © Jan Butchofsky-Houser/CORBIS
p.4    Beaked Heliconia © Jonathan Blair/CORBIS
p.5    Sunrise viewed from Mount Hillaby © Tony Arruza/CORBIS
p.6    Sunset in Barbados © Torleif Svensson/CORBIS
p.16   Parasailer © CORBIS
p.31   Aerial view of Mustique, St Vincent and the Grenadines © Yann Arthus-Bertrand/CORBIS
p.31   Rum cocktails © Jonathan Blair/CORBIS
p.36   Scuba divers at sunken Greek freight ship the *Stavronikita* near Barbados © Karl Weatherly/CORBIS
p.37   US amateur surfer Damien Hobgood © Rick Doyle/CORBIS

p.37   Snorkeller off Barbados © Buddy Mays/CORBIS
p.40   Holetown Festival parade © Jonathan Blair/CORBIS
p.41   England's Graham Thorpe and West Indies' Tino Best at Kensington Oval © Andy Clark/CORBIS
p.41   Barbados Jazz Festival © Barbados Tourist Board
p.41   Crop Over Festival dancers © Dave G. Houser/CORBIS
p.44   Striped Grunt © Larry Williams/CORBIS
p.45   Blue marlin © Tony Arruza/CORBIS
p.45   Hummingbird © Ron Sanford/CORBIS
p.45   Diver feeding sea turtle © Torleif Svensson/CORBIS
p.47   Road tennis © Barbados Tourist Board
p.48   Closed window shutters, Bridgetown © Richard Cummino/CORBIS

INDEX

# Index

INDEX